Interactive Visual Ideas for Musical Classroom Activities

Interactive Visual Ideas for Musical Classroom Activities

Tips for Music Teachers

Catherine Dwinal

OXFORD
UNIVERSITY PRESS

Oxford University Press is a department of the University of Oxford. It furthers the University's objective of excellence in research, scholarship, and education by publishing worldwide. Oxford is a registered trade mark of Oxford University Press in the UK and certain other countries.

Published in the United States of America by Oxford University Press
198 Madison Avenue, New York, NY 10016, United States of America.

Library of Congress Cataloging-in-Publication Data
Names: Dwinal, Catherine, author.
Title: Interactive visual ideas for musical classroom activities :
tips for music teachers / Catherine Dwinal.
Description: New York : Oxford University Press, 2020. |
Series: Essential music technology: The prestissimo series |
Includes bibliographical references and index.
Identifiers: LCCN 2020007948 (print) | LCCN 2020007949 (ebook) |
ISBN 9780190929855 (hardback) | ISBN 9780190929862 (paperback) |
ISBN 9780190929886 (epub)
Subjects: LCSH: Music—Instruction and study—Technological innovations. |
Music—Instruction and study—Audio-visual aids.
Classification: LCC MT1 .D88 2020 (print) | LCC MT1 (ebook) |
DDC 780.71—dc23
LC record available at https://lccn.loc.gov/2020007948
LC ebook record available at https://lccn.loc.gov/2020007949

9 8 7 6 5 4 3 2 1

Paperback printed by Marquis, Canada
Hardback printed by Bridgeport National Bindery, Inc., United States of America

To my friends and mentors, thank you for the encouragement always to be learning, growing, and sharing. I would not be where I am today in my career without you.

To my family, thank you for listening, thank you for encouraging, and thank you for helping me get through!

Contents

Foreword

A blank screen is magical--a white canvas waiting for an explosion of color with ink or paint, a fresh snowfall waiting for the first crunchy footsteps, a clean tablecloth waiting for a sumptuous dinner setting and a delicious meal.

Those of us "of a certain age" remember back to the joy of walking into an elementary school music room and finding a TV set up. As soon as you saw that screen, you knew it was about to be the best class ever. Sometimes you got to watch educational programs about famous composers, sometimes a movie version of *Peter and the Wolf* or *Tubby the Tuba*, sometimes fun musical cartoons like "What's Opera, Doc?" or "The Cat Concerto." Those were, undeniably, the best classes ever, because your mind could be carried away from the school walls to distant destinations, transported and inspired by waves of beautiful music. It wasn't just the visual element of the screen that was so engaging, it was the entire audio/visual immersion--a "dream come true" for all we young aspiring musicians.

Then came high school, and the screen became unmagical. Many times the sight of a screen in the classroom preceded slides of facts and dates parroted unenthusiastically by an instructor who seemed to have become more lecturer than musical mentor. The screen, and presentation software, had become a shortcut for delivering instruction without any room for discussion or alteration of content. Because the slides had been pre-prepared, it was obvious that this class was only going one direction, and each of the students had already worked out what that direction was by observing the objective on the board. We felt betrayed. The screen, which so few years ago had promised magical enchantment, now offered little more than educational paralysis and an hour of sitting quietly in a chair listening to someone read out notes that any of us could have read ourselves in a few minutes.

Alas, any of us who have sat in a professional development meeting where the first words said were "I have a slideshow for you" know all too well how visual presentation software has sadly become the most badly used of all technological developments of the last thirty years. We see how the once- magical screen has become representative of ennui and we swear to get away from screens as much as possible in our own work.

Thomas Aquinas's philosophy taught us that nothing in the w orld is inherently good or evil, but that it is its manner of usage that may make it so. This is unfortunately true of the screen and of visual presentations. The screen and the software are not to blame for our current "paralysis by presentation" epidemic, rather it is the unskilled and unimaginative presenter that turns something with so much potential into something so dull.

Music teachers are used to making things magical—we do it every day. Every time a child walks into a music classroom, they are inspired by the potential of what is to happen that day. Every lesson should be the best class ever. So, it should come as no surprise that music teachers are often the best at using screens and visual software. When an adult walks into a music classroom to see students actively engaged with software on an inter- active whiteboard, making and enjoying music through software titles such as Quaver Music or the interactive elements of the Music First suite, they are thrilled and overjoyed to see that the screen has become the catalyst for the magic.

Those teachers who are incredibly skilled at using the myriad of current presen- tation options (interactive projectors, document cameras, SMART boards, et al.) are those who recognize that the tools enhance and bring out the magic in what is already there—the music. They know that the potential goes beyond their imagination, and so, not in-coincidentally, they are the ones who are often looking to other teachers for ad- vice, borrowing ideas from each other at conferences and PD days, sharing successes and do-overs online, keeping pace with a technology that seems to grow even faster than the kids.

Catie Dwinal is a pioneer in the use of interactive visual techniques in her classroom. She began her career teaching elementary students in New Hampshire and found every way possible to enhance and modernize her classroom, making music classes the high- light of every day for every student. Her incredible work led her to become the youngest ever recipient of the TI:ME (Technology In Music Education) Teacher of the Year Award, in 2014, at the tender age of twenty-six years old. Catie now tours the United States and abroad as a representative for Quaver Music, and she presents at many state and national music conferences. Her presentations are remarkable. Yes, when you go in you'll see that magical blank screen, but pretty soon she'll have you up dancing, making music, and loving life. Imagine what it would be like to be a student in her classroom every day.

It is in that vein and that spirit that Ms. Dwinal has chosen to present many of her ideas to you in this volume. This book passes the magic of her experience on to you. The following pages are organized in such a way as to allow you to dip in and find fun and educationally appropriate activities for your classroom, no matter what age you teach or what equipment you have access to. Each of these lesson ideas and classroom hints have been proven to work successfully, and even just incorporating one or two of them into your lesson plans each semester will make your classroom a haven of musical joy. Our hope is that you will be inspired to use what you already have in new ways, and that your students will be the true beneficiaries of the superb material presented here.

Richard McCready
Series Editor

Introduction

When I began teaching, I decided to incorporate digital methods into my style of instruction. This was one of the things that my students remember most about our time together in class. I didn't have many resources when I started, nor did I want to; it would have been too overwhelming to have everything I wanted right off the bat.

I was new and had to learn how to be a teacher before I could start to explore different methods of instruction. Most of my first year was spent incorporating a projector and a computer into my classroom and finding the thousands of uses for only those two tools. It was just the first step in the adventure, because you can go beyond using the system merely to show a picture or a website.

There are, of course, many times where I do use it to play short videos, show pictures, and explore websites because that is what fits my lesson that day. Then there are times that I bring up interactive field trips, spinning the globe on Google Maps to show students different parts of the world. Even though it would be amazing to have an interactive projector, I'm not above asking students to point to the screen and pretend to drag and drop as I moved the targets with my computer mouse.

Think about it from an SAMR perspective, the education substitution, augmentation, modification, and redefinition technology implementation framework from Dr. Puentedura.[1] I started by doing just simple substitutions like this before moving to augmenting and beyond. It was a way to take a traditional pedagogy and add a dash of twenty-first-century instruction to it, to engage the digital natives I had sitting in the classroom and relate what we did in class to their daily lives.

---

1. Puentedura, R. (2014, December 11). "SAMR and TPCK: A Hands-On Approach to Classroom Practice." Retrieved from http://www.hippasus.com/rrpweblog/archives/2014_12.html

Interactive Visual Ideas for Musical Classroom Activities. Catherine Dwinal, Oxford University Press (2020). © Oxford University Press.
DOI: 10.1093/oso/9780190929855.001.0001

As the years moved on and I became more comfortable teaching students, I started to add more resources and experiment more in-depth with the system I had. When I finally got an iPad, I began to use it to remotely access the desktop from my computer and became untethered from the front of the room. This tool allowed me to be able to immerse myself more into what was happening beyond the front of the classroom. I could sit with students and play the recorder with them, with the ability to start, stop, and change the music whenever I needed.

Incorporating just one new piece of technology into my instruction seemed so daunting, but it was so simple once I started and it became a staple in my room. It doesn't matter how low- or high-tech it is. It's all about how you use it.

That is where my journey began. I wanted to figure out the best ways to use what I had and share it with others. I talked with coaches, shared with friends, and learned as much as I could from peers and mentors.

A projection system can very much be considered the center of the classroom. It can be the first thing a student sees when they walk through the door, and the last thing students experience before they leave. It is also the only piece of technology a music educator may have in their classroom. I cannot tell you how many times over the recent years I have heard, "They are getting me a projector! I've never had one before."

A projection system is an active part of the instruction that allows students to practice digital skills and allows the teacher to provide engaging visuals for today's digital learner. You can now share pictures and videos with the whole class at one time without having to take the time out of your busy day to print out and pass around an image, or have the class crowd around you to look at your monitor. Students can all follow along while playing simple songs and warm-ups, practicing their listening skills, or playing in an ensemble. You can truly meet the needs of all the visual learners in your classroom who might struggle with not being able to visualize concepts you are talking about during class.

According to the Visual Teaching Alliance, 65 percent of the world's population are visual learners (http://visualteachingalliance.com). Although we have been used to teaching orally for so long, most of the current society does not learn this way. A projection system in your room gives you a tool that can help students to understand what you are explaining, and in cases like the interactive board, students can engage with it as well.

Students have a decreased attention span due to the content they are now consuming, from 6-second videos to the 25,600 short ads they see a year.[2]

The ways that current students learn are different than what they were even ten years ago. The use of simple technology tools helps to connect the dots and engage students' revved-up brains toward more educational discovery. Take some of that screen time they would use to meander around the Internet and change their perspective: teach

---

2. Moses, L. (2014, March 11). "A Look at Kid's' Exposure to Ads." Retrieved from https://www.adweek.com/digital/look-kids-exposure-ads-156191/

them to use the tools as a way to create and expand knowledge instead of merely consuming what is readily at their fingertips. A critical point to spotlight is that technology has begun to change us from consumers to creators.

It has begun to adjust our educational core values from reciting facts and figures to creating content, providing real-world application, and challenging problem-solving skills. It shows an evolution in the way that we teach and prepares our students for the future. Careers have been changing over the decades as our culture has evolved and matured with the growth of technology and with education being initially the system to prepare students for future careers. This change needed to happen to continue to prepare those students for their futures.

Even though it is tough at times for teachers to acquire the resources they want, any technology they bring into their rooms allows a chance for students to build their proficiency and skills for the road ahead. If the teacher is using technology for instructional methods only and it is not interactive, students can still learn by example. Do you know the phrase "They are always watching"? That stands true here. Students also learn about how to use technology on their own by watching the teacher.

Having a projection system in the room also allows for the teacher to work on their own technology literacy as they learn to use and integrate it, problem-solve different issues, and elevate their daily routines using the available resources. Teachers also work on their critical thinking skills as they put together how they want to upgrade their lessons and keep learning new and fresh with the continually evolving student audience. It also assists them with their own threshold for patience and flexibility as well as teaching students that it is always okay to fail at trying something new as long as you get back up and try again. Using systems like a projector or an interactive board for small tasks might seem like no big deal, but the way you use it and the more you use it in different ways can make a big difference in the end.

Having a projection system has become so crucial pedagogically because it is one of the best ways to differentiate instruction by giving your visual learners a way to see the concepts you are teaching and provide more interactivity for your kinetic learners. It also meet our students where they are in this technology-driven world. Having such a system is now almost a requirement for every classroom. Having a system can make your life as an educator easier through more organizational options and less time precious time spent making the visuals. Projection systems have become an important tool that has changed the design and delivery of instruction for the better.

You might be asking, "Which one is the best? Which type of system should I get?" To be truthful, I cannot tell you which one is the best or which one you should have because it depends on a lot of different factors, from your teaching style to your classroom set-up. You also might have to have your district technology department choose for you based on what will work best for the district's network. Be open to any system; you can do so much with anything that is out there. It just takes a little creativity.

FIGURE 1.1 Demonstrating to students the power of an interactive board. (Photo Credit C. Dwinal)

In this publication, you will discover ideas, resources, and hopefully, motivation to continue creating more experiences like the ones presented to you in this book. Do not think of this as a curriculum. Think of it more as your own instructional tech coach here to specifically cater to your projection system needs in the music room. Challenge yourself to step out of what is comfortable.

We teach students that it is okay to fail if you are willing to stand back up and try again. To best teach that, we need to be role models for it ourselves—do what we think is impossible and persist until we make it possible. Those of us who stay in our comfort zones and do not try to step outside the circle never get to experience the innovations that lie out there.

As educators, we always need to be growing and changing. If we don't, there is a chance of being stuck and losing the sense of what motivates us to teach the next generation to change the world. To step beyond our circles, we need to be able to let our inhibitions and doubts go and be flexible if there are times when something doesn't work out the way we want. Knowing that and being confident in the face of those challenges makes a huge difference.

There are many things that a teacher has to consider when teaching, from the audience, the equipment, learners' needs, what knowledge they come into class with, etc. If you can take that and create a memorable experience for your students in which they learn and walk out of your room still talking about it, then you've done something special. You stepped outside of your comfort zone and said "Yes." You were creative, you were open-minded, and you most likely motivated your students to continue to learn and grow.

When it comes to technology, you do not have to use the flashiest things to do what you want to do. You could begin with something small, and then as you take more and more steps outside of your comfort circle, the creative juices start to flow more, and you begin to think outside the box and go from developing "lessons" to developing "learning experiences." So think big and start small.

The purpose of this publication is to use it as a reference that you, as an educator, can utilize to pick and choose activities that will best suit your instruction. The chapters are organized by device type, and the lessons in each chapter are organized by grade level and level of difficulty. Pick and choose lessons in each chapter based on the device you have and the grade levels you want to use it with.

Choose activities to incorporate into your lessons that best fit your level of comfort with using technology in your classroom. Choose a few that you could do right now and some that you can try later after you've become more comfortable. Then start! (If you need a different tool to use with the activity, go to the Resources Index and find ways to substitute within the lesson.)

Consider this resource as your technology coach. Not every classroom is the same; not every teacher is the same; and not every group of students is the same. Use this book as a reference and a guide to new ideas where you can pick and choose what will work for you. Know that this publication is here to give you ideas and guide you as you integrate such essential tools into your lessons to meet the needs of your digitally engaged audience.

Tips to Get Started

Teach Yourself Enough

There are times when we want to be entirely in control and know everything before we present it to our audience. In reality, though, we will never know enough to ever be truly prepared. Learn the basics of how to use your system and especially how to do basic troubleshooting.

You will be surprised how much you will learn on the job. Before you try something out in your lessons, make sure you know how to get it started and ready to go. Know the essential tools like calibrating, using the draw tools (if it is an interactive board), also adjusting the picture if needed.

Know That There Will Be Times You Will Have Malfunctions

Not everything is going to be perfect the first, the second, or even the third time. There are still times where I am hoping and praying that everything does not die on me during a lesson. You will always see me with backup plans, and I say plans in plural because you might have to get to plan E before something works.

You can teach your students that even when something goes wrong, it is best to stay calm to be able to fix it. Just stay calm and troubleshoot and know where to go if you have tried it all and it does not fix the problem. Then, if all else fails, pick yourself up, change gears, and move on.

Bake Your IT Cookies!

First, know who your IT department is and what they do. They are the ones who help you when basic troubleshooting does not fix the issues. It might be a unique issue only they have the tools to fix, or it might be a network issue, which could be bigger trouble.

They, most of the time, will be willing to set you up with the newest gear, fix any problems you may have, and help to integrate the tech into your classroom. It always helps to bring them a treat as well! Think of this team like you do your secretary or even the custodial staff. Those departments help you with scheduling and performances. IT helps you with your tools in class.

Practice the Basics Before the Kids Get There

This tip goes along with knowing the basics before you use your new systems with students. It is one thing to "know," but another thing to "do." Practice with your materials.

Invite a friend to come into your room a few days before school, and both of you explore what you want to do with the machine. Make sure you know how everything works and that all of your devices have sufficient power. If you feel like you need some real fun, have each of your friends practice being the teacher while the others are the students and go through a few lessons using the board.

Not Everything Can Be Fixed in a Day

Not everything can get resolved right away. You might have to wait a few days for a new bulb to come in, or the Internet might be experiencing issues all across the district, and you might be out of luck for the day. The technology we use will fail us every once in a while, but it is still something that helps us, and we need to be patient with what we have. Make sure to alert your IT as soon as something malfunctions. The faster you do, the faster it gets on their list, and your class gets back up and running more quickly.

Always Set the Rules First with Kids

Consider building in rules for technology use in your classroom at the beginning of the year. Set down those expectations and procedures just like you would with standard rules in your class. Students do not inherently know how to act with technology and need to be taught what to do.

If they know that when it is time to use Chromebooks or laptops they need to use them on the tables or have them sitting flat on the floor, then make sure they practice and understand that. The rules that I always set down for my students when using the projector system are:

- You need to sit at least two bodies back from the wall.
- Keep an aisle down the middle so people can come up and take turns.
- Touch the board or device gently.
- Be patient.
- Take turns; let everyone get a chance.

I, of course, have slightly different rules when it comes to mobile devices and such, but the students know how to handle them and understand the expectations that are laid down from the beginning. If they know that what they have is unique it will help them learn and have fun. Then they take using what they have more seriously and keep the devices in better shape. Treat it as a learning experience!

Be Okay with Students Taking the Lead

Instruction is changing, and it is time to share that spotlight with your students. It's your turn to be the facilitator and guide of knowledge rather than the "sage on the stage." Whether it is to help with a warm-up or to teach their classmates what they learned, this helps them develop confidence, encourages them to be a more active part of their learning, and of course, builds leadership skills. So, make time to let students do some of the leading. It helps create a more collaborative environment!

It Is Okay to Use Technology in a Small Group or for Whole Classwork

Your projection system is essential. It is a significant fixture in the music room that most teachers will build their space around. The fact of the matter is that even though it is a large part of your area, not all students need to use it at the same time. For instance, during center time one group of your students could do an activity on the board, or use it for small ensemble practice; one of the groups could use the system to play along with certain parts of the music. There are so many ways to be able to use the system; do not limit it to just one way of instruction.

It Is Healthy to Turn Your Back to It

Make sure to balance your screen time in lessons to leave room for all the singing, dancing, and playing you want to do. Using technology is only a small part of everything. Avoid being glued to it the whole time.

Use it for an activity, then get up and move around. You could also incorporate it into creating or composing music. Jump back and forth in a lesson and use the system where it can enhance the learning.

Keep It Clean

Make sure that you maintain it to last as long as possible. Keeping it clean means you need to make sure it is wiped down periodically to be free of dirt and grime. Make sure to keep any other fabrics or materials away from the devices.

Most importantly, shut it off at the end of the day or during any long breaks during the school day. Don't leave it on all the time or the bulbs or batteries in the devices burn out a lot faster than the recommended wear and tear.

You *Can* Be Untethered!

Walk away from the front of the room and be a part of the action with your students. A cheap way to do this is to get a $10 wireless mouse from your nearest office supply store and carry that with you. There are other methods of communicating wirelessly with your system, from SMART Slates to using a mobile device like an iPad. I love using an a pp called Splashtop to remotely access my computer's desktop and be able to control it from anywhere in the room!

Always Have a Plan B

After plan B, have plans C through Z ready as well because you most likely will need them at some point. I still have other plans of action up my sleeve just in case I have a bad day and the technology doesn't work. Always be ready to roll with the punches and do not be afraid to be adventurous and get messy! You never know what kinds of things will happen during the school day with your students, and it's the same with technology. It can be unpredictable.

Know What to Troubleshoot First

Always have an essential troubleshooting checklist.

- Did you turn it off and on (reboot)?
- Did you make sure everything is plugged in correctly?
- Is the Internet working?
- Have you tried a different web browser?
- Is your software up to date?

Sometimes just going down that list can solve your problem quickly!

Tricks

Blank Screen

This is a perfect trick for those wandering eyes that cannot help but stare at whatever pretty colors and moving objects that are in front of them. On a Windows machine, if you hold down the Windows and D key it will quickly turn your screen black. On a Mac, if you choose Control-Shift-Power, it will put the computer to sleep; hit any key on the keyboard to wake it back up quickly.

Use this if you want to hide something on the board for an activity. You might also have students who cannot pay attention to you while you are discussing a topic, so you need to turn off the screen to regain their attention. Is also a perfect way to get something prepared before class on the board to use later.

Extending the Display

On a PC, you need to right-click on the desktop and click Screen Resolution, then Multiple Displays, and Extend These Displays. To extend it on a Mac computer you need to head into System Preferences, then Displays; after that click on the Extend the Display to create a giant screen using two displays. This way, you can put what you want to show to the audience on one side where it is projecting to the class while the other can have your tools that are for the teacher's eyes only.

Mirroring a Display

Most of the time, when you first hook up your projector or display, you make sure that it is set to "On" in the Settings. On a PC, you right-click on the desktop and click Screen Resolution, then Multiple Displays, and make sure that Extend These Displays is unchecked. To mirror it on a Mac computer you need go to System Preferences, then Displays; after that make sure the Extend the Display box is unchecked.

Calibrating Touch Points on Your Board a Little Offset?

This is most likely due to the calibration not being set correctly. If you have an interactive display on wheels or one with a projector on an arm that is prone to shake around a lot due to lots of movement, then you need to calibrate it regularly. I always recommend getting interactive boards and projectors permanently mounted to a wall to reduce the frequency of calibrating your system.

The exact calibration process depends on the system you have. For the sake of staying with ever-changing technology, you will need to refer back to the manufacturer's manual for directions on how to do so. It is normal to calibrate once a week or once every other week. When you do calibrate, make sure to use a small pointer when touching the points on a screen. Calibrating will be more accurate and make the board more comfortable to use because the touch points will be more responsive.

Drawing on an Interactive Display

Tip number one: Do not use an actual marker on your projection system, dry erase or otherwise. It will haunt you by creating marks on your displays that will never go away. There are usually pens that come with SMART Boards and Promethean displays.

If your system did not come with pens, you can use things like a stylus or a teacher's board pointer. There are styluses made in a larger width meant for little hands. Make sure the stylus or pointer is rubber-based. It mimics the human touch the best and allows for better interactivity on the board.

Adjusting the Screen for Odd Angles

Sometimes you'll want to are set up your projector in an angle other than a straight-on projection. You should find two buttons on the menu that allow you to keystone the picture. This tool will adjust the image up and down, and left and right, to create the best square for the angle you have it. You most likely will not have keystoning on a TV display but will have a screen resolution setting that will allow you to make the picture bigger or smaller and adjust the size of the icons and images on the screen in front of you.

Screen Clarity

The projector distance is vital for the best screen size and clarity. On most projectors, there are two turn dials on the front of the projector where the lens is. One fixes your blurry screen, and the other helps to make the screen smaller or larger to a certain amount. Also, if you are like me and are a little perfectionistic, you can better fill in the white space on your board with the picture coming from your projector to fill out the space.

Turn Out front Lights

If it is hard for your students to see your projection system in the front of the room, then you may need to adjust the classroom's lighting. Perhaps the bulb is getting ready to die and is projecting a softer picture, or the board the image is projected on is not the best for this use. Turn off the front row of lights in your room to see it more comfortably. It will be better for the picture but also better for your eyes.

I-Can-Do-This-Tomorrows

When you first start using a new piece of technology, it is hard to figure out where to begin. You have a lot to do and not a ton of time to experiment to find activities that would easily fit into your daily instruction. Just remember, you do not have to overcomplicate things.

As you are reading this book, take away one new tip or one unique activity that you know you can do tomorrow, and you are ready to take on the challenge. These are great little ways to build up your knowledge and confidence as you start to work toward longer-term goals of using technology in your music room. Take some of the following suggestions; incorporate them into your daily instruction as you work with the projects and activities included in this publication. It will make it easier to plan and follow through with using your projection system more in your daily lessons.

1. **Use it to share visuals.** This activity is one of the most effective uses of a projection system in a classroom. There are four different types of learners: auditory, reading and writing, kinesthetic, and visual. When lesson planning, you have to take into account that you will have every kind of learner in each of your classes and have to provide activities that fit every type of learning style. Posters and printed pictures are acceptable, but projected images can be seen better by the whole class, they can be easily stored for multiple uses and edited for specific needs, and most of the time they can be interactive.

You can keep a folder of pictures to use in lessons throughout the year (make sure to label them so you can always find them). Or if you like to do things off-the-cuff, go to Google and find an image in the search feature that fits what you are talking about at that moment. This way, as you speak about a topic such as the string family, you can show students pictures of the actual instruments on the board.

Interactive Visual Ideas for Musical Classroom Activities. Catherine Dwinal, Oxford University Press (2020). © Oxford University Press.
DOI: 10.1093/oso/9780190929855.001.0001

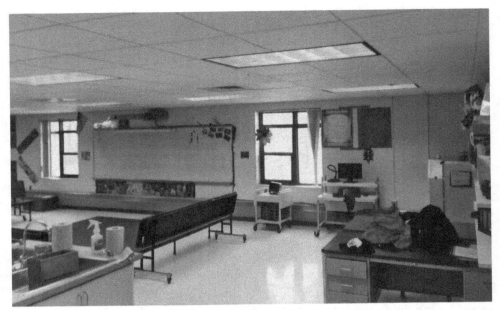

FIGURE 2.1 I had my system up at the front of the room with the chairs surrounding the system. (Photo Credit C. Dwinal)

2. **Show videos!** Later on, in this book, you will find more activities like this but a little more in-depth. Showing a clip of a video is a simple activity that can help enhance any lesson. It is not the process of playing a video for the entire class period, but having small clips, that enhance the teaching. When I am teaching a lesson, I always make sure to have one or two short clips in my bag of tricks as a way to give a different perspective on the topic. Use Vimeo or YouTube to search for a short clip that enhances your lesson. It could be a DJ talking about the history of hip-hop, or a luthier talking about what goes into building a guitar.

3. **Use the projector speakers for music.** In most projection systems there are speakers that you can use—not optimal if you are looking for the best sound quality, but great in a pinch. Projectors and interactive displays are the most likely to have them while document cameras and streaming media players rely on different systems to play sound. If you have a projector or interactive board though, you do have the option of plugging in to play your music if the speaker situation in the room is less than ideal. There are usually tools on the devices themselves like "Eco Screen" or "Blank Screen" that can hide the picture as the music plays.

4. **Do research together!** Teachable moments happen in a class all the time. Using search engines like Google or Bing, or more kid-friendly search engines like Kiddle or KidRex, can be easy to jump on when a student has a question. Putting it up on your board allows for the whole class to contribute to discussions that are going on in the group.

5. **Project a PDF of a Score.** We go a little deeper later in this book, but I wanted to make sure to stress the importance and ease of this activity in the music room. Take one of your scores and scan it into the computer (your copy machine in the teacher's lounge most likely can scan to a USB key or into an email). Project it for the class to see. This is perfect for general music class needs or even warm-ups and sight-reading in an ensemble rehearsal. If you are using an interactive display, you can usually use the writing utensils to mark up the score to highlight parts that need to be focused on or played again by the students.

Projectors

Websites with Visual Material

Recommended Grades: PreK–12
Difficulty: Beginner
Time: 5–30 min.
Objective: Students will practice and reinforce learned concepts by viewing online or interactive visual materials.

Resources
- Computer
- Projector
- Speakers
- Website of choice (see resource index for suggestions)

This activity can be an easy one to do in class, but also one of the hardest to plan because of the vast amount of options available to us. In my lessons I use a very long list of websites. Thanks to social media, that list keeps growing. It is always a difficult task to find the right website to fit the lesson, but when I find one, it becomes an experience that the kids remember. I love it when I have students ask me to write down the site for them so they can go home and play on it. I have made a habit of putting all the websites we use in class on my class website after we use them, so students have a shortcut! I have a website for almost every kind of instruction and tangent known to man! It is a part of my teaching arsenal that I use as interactive visuals for students during many lessons.

Before Class
- Make sure you have a website that fits the purpose of the lesson. Don't show something just because it's cool. You want something that is either going to be an engaging visual

Interactive Visual Ideas for Musical Classroom Activities. Catherine Dwinal, Oxford University Press (2020). © Oxford University Press.
DOI: 10.1093/oso/9780190929855.001.0001

or resource that will contribute to the instruction, or an interactive activity that will reinforce the learning.

- o Some suggestions on where to start:
  - Using Google Earth, show students where the music they are performing originated! If they are learning about the blues, show them Memphis, Tennessee. If you are working on a piece from New Zealand for a concert, show them around that country so they can get a better understanding of the culture and geography.
  - You can use a website like Noteflight as you are discussing the building blocks of a composition to visually show students how they work when put together on a staff.
  - During a unit on the science of sound, take a website like Chrome Music Lab to show your students a spectrogram or oscillator that provides a visual of sound waves.
- On the day of class, make sure to double-check your Internet connection and go to the website to make sure it works correctly! (Remember to check the sound too!)

During Class

- Incredibox.com is an interactive website that allows students to build vocal ostinato groups to create in-depth pieces of music. Have students explore the different sounds and then choose voices to make those sounds. Then create music as a class.
- MusicTheory.net has simple games that reinforce music theory concepts and do not take up a lot of time. Bring up an activity like the note naming exercises and have students work together to answer the questions.
- Use http://www.virtualmusicalinstruments.com to demonstrate different aspects of the instrument. Bring up the keyboard during a piano unit to best demonstrate proper fingering and best ways to play certain melodies.
- Try to present students with a list of notable composers from all musical periods. Go to https://classicsforkids.com/ and click on Composers and then Composer Timeline. Students can work together to divide a list of composers they have in front of them by musical period. They can draw their own timelines on paper, either in groups or individually. This activity is excellent for reinforcing when composers lived and what the different musical periods are.

Assessment Tips:

- Using Incredibox, assess your students on their practical application of form and phrasing as they build their vocal ostinatos.
- Have students bring up MusicTheory.net on their own devices and go to the exercises. Choose the task you want them to work on and have them try to get their best score out of 25. Have students screenshot their scores and send them to you.

- Using Classicsforkids.com, assess students on their knowledge of composers by time period.

Brainstorming Activities

Recommended Grades: PreK–12

    Difficulty: Beginner

    Time: 5–30 min.

    Objective: To build critical thinking and improve skills through brainstorming activities presented on the board.

Resources
- Computer
- Projector
- Speakers
- Website suggestions: https://awwapp.com/#, https://padlet.com/dashboard, http://popplet.com

One of the best ways you can use a projector and board is to have your class collaborate and see each other's ideas. There are great tools out there that take brainstorming beyond writing ideas on a whiteboard and allow you to create mind maps and savable products that can show the beginning stages of the creative process. We do brainstorming activities all of the time in class. I pose a question or give students a theme to spend a few minutes thinking about before doing a giant discussion together about everything we knew or thought about the subject. I teach my students during this time that there is no wrong answer as long as they try. (I don't accept solutions that apparently required no effort or were meant for disrupting the class.)

Before Class
- Double-check your Internet connection to make sure everything is running.
  - If you suspect your Internet might be having an issue, go to https://fast.com, and do an Internet speed test. The more Mbps (megabits per second) you have, the better. If you have anything under 6 Mbps, then it is time to contact your tech department to have your Internet connection checked out.
- Make sure the tools you want to use are compatible with your school computer. This tip means that you need to test it on the computer you will be using for the class to make sure it all works together.

- On the day of class, bring up the tool that you are going to use on your computer, so you have it ready to use.
- Test it to make sure that it is still working for the class.

During Class

- To save precious whiteboard space and to have a place to keep all the brainstorming work, use a whiteboard app such as https://awwapp.com/#. Ask a question or propose a problem that needs solving. Have students add their thoughts to the board. Then discuss what their answers to the problem could be. Is there an ongoing theme?
- This activity is especially useful if you have a 1:1 ratio of devices to students as well as a projector. Head to Padlet.com and create a Padlet space that is specific to what you are discussing. Share the link with students, who can then access it from their mobile devices (or use a computer connected to the projector and take turns) and post to the discussion. They then can respond to their classmates' posts or a conversation you have started. Padlet is also another platform that students can use to ask you questions without the terror of having to raise their hands.
- Popplet.com is a mind mapping tool that allows the user to create a brainstorming map. Choose a topic such as a composer like Mozart or a musical style like hip-hop and have students add facts to the mind map and organize them accordingly.
- Some suggestions for brainstorming starters:
  o How many instruments can we name?
  o What did rock 'n' roll do for the music we know today?
  o What composers do we know from the classical period?
  o Listen to the piece. What do you think the composer was trying to tell the listener?
  o What pieces of classical music can we name?

Assessment Tip: Assess students on how they participate in the class brainstorming activities.

Background Projection

Recommended Grades: PreK–12
Difficulty: Beginner
Time: 15 min.–1 hr. 30 min.
Objective: Students will utilize projectable images to reinforce the subject of their performance or project.

Resources

- Computer
- Projector

- PowerPoint
- Google Images

You can use the power of the projector for different projects. We did a project one year that was cross-curricular and data-driven. I worked with my colleagues in PE and media to develop videos about the history of dance with the students. Students researched, wrote music, and choreographed a routine together. They also found images to use as they performed. When it came time to film everything, we cleared out my room and projected their chosen images in the background as they danced. This setup is also an easy way to get a green screen going! Instead of projecting a picture, put up a green background. Back projection is also a great way to have a clean backdrop projected during a show (Put the projector behind a thin screen and flip the image.) Way back in the day, when I was younger, my mom ran an American sign language chorus. I did technical projects for her to add something cool to the show. One year we pulled a white sheet tight over a wooden frame, then put a projector behind it and flipped the picture of Kermit the Frog singing "Rainbow Connection." It was a clean background, and a visual spectacle on stage added to the stage decor as the students signed to the song.

Before Class

- Choose images for your backdrop and put them into a PowerPoint presentation to save to your computer. You can put a bunch of backgrounds together to change back and forth quickly.
- Make sure the background you are projecting on is solid white, for optimal projection. If needed, hang a thick white cloth.
- Also, check your projector bulb. If you have not changed it in a while, you may have a duller picture.
- Try getting a green screen background ready as well. Using an app like Do Ink, you can edit videos. You can get green art paper from the giant rolls your art teacher most likely will have, or you can head to your local fabric store and get a thick piece of green fabric to hang on your wall for this activity.
- On the day of class, adjust the lighting in your room to bring out the best of the backgrounds. I usually go darker in the front of the room and lighter toward the back.
- Turn up the brightness on your projector. (You can find these controls either on the projector itself or the remote.)
- Make sure to pull up the pictures you will need to project for the activity.
- It would be easiest if you placed the projector on the floor and shot it upward. That way, students can be in front of the projector and not get in its way.

During Class (or Performance!)

- Use these backgrounds as part of a project. Have students plan videos as final products of what they might be learning. For example, if a student is doing a research project on a composer, have them prepare a video about that composer with background on where that composer lived or their primary instrument. Have the students act out that video in front of that background. Bonus: Put together a reel of all the student's videos and have a movie day!

- Use the backgrounds for your instruction. Put yourself in space before you introduce a song about Pluto. Have a marching band back you up as you introduce John Phillip Sousa. You could even take students on a journey to a different country to help immerse them in the song you are teaching from that culture. This activity especially helps differentiate your instruction. You are meeting the needs of the visual learners in your room with a simple picture and are engaging everyone as you discuss the topic at hand.

- Another activity you could do is project images onto a screen behind your performers for an upcoming performance. This trick will allow you to create scenes that you

FIGURE 3.1 I have a cart setup that I could roll around into performances (Photo Credit C. Dwinal)

usually could not paint on a backdrop. Be careful not to get the light in performers' eyes. (I learned this the hard way one year!) If necessary, borrow a short-throw or ultra-short-throw projector to put the projector closer to the screen and still keep a big picture. If that is not an option, try to place the projector on a higher mounting arm so it is above the performers, or in an area where they will not cross in front.

Assessment Tip: As you assess the student's overall performance or video creation, include criteria that consider how the student used the background in their performance. Was it the right choice for the performance? Did it contribute to the message they were trying to get across?

Noise Meter

Recommended Grades: K–5
   Difficulty: Beginner
   Time: 5–10 min.
   Objective: Students will identify loud and soft dynamics through visual representations projected on the board.

Resources
- Computer
- Projector
- Speakers
- https://bouncyballs.org

Noise meters are a great tool, not only for classroom management, but also for dynamics work and even adding some science. There are several variations of noise meters among the many available. Bouncyballs.org has several different types of bouncing objects, from balls to eyeballs, that can capture students' attention. Having a noise meter like Bouncy Balls helps students understand how loud they can be in the class and work on their dynamics language at the same time! It can also be a tool for teaching younger students about the different types of voices that they use every day. If they are whispering, then the balls will not move much, but if they are yelling, then the balls will go crazy!

Before Class
- Make sure you have the noise meter bookmarked to get to it quickly. I highly suggest that you load it up before the students come in. This trick will also prevent any slow loading issues which can cause unfortunate dead time during class.
- Test out your microphone. If you have a newer computer, you most likely have one built in. If you do not have a microphone then you will need to get one or ask your IT to purchase one for you. This is an essential tool to have for any music classroom.

I suggest looking for a USB mic. I have found much success with a Blue Snowball mic, but it is your or your IT's decision as to what will work best for your computer. You will need to have a microphone that will be omnidirectional, to better pick up the ambient room sounds.

During Class

- There are several very different ways you can use this resource. The first and most straightforward way is to reduce the noise level in class, especially with a rowdier group of students. Challenge them to keep the balls from bouncing as soon as they walk into the room. If they make the balls bounce then have them go out of the room and practice coming back in again and again until they understand what the noise level should be. It will help them better understand the expectations placed on them. Once they know what the acceptable noise level feels like, they will know how to come in calmly the next time. Sometimes you have to do things like this over and over with students but once they finally nail it, it becomes easier for them to do it. You might also have certain parts of the class, like centers or small group work, where the noise becomes deafening in your room, and you need to work on keeping the noise level down. Keeping this on the board will give students visual cues as to where their noise level is.
- Another way to use the noise meter is to work on dynamics during ensemble rehearsals. I have to go over dynamic markings with my ensembles repeatedly. Sometimes I describe a marking and students respond with blank looks on their faces. They need a visual to understand how loud or how soft I require them to be during individual sections. Pick out specific parts in the music they are rehearsing and have them keep an eye on the bouncing balls as they are practicing. If they are too soft, have them adjust and play, so the balls bounce higher. Or maybe they are too loud, so they need to work at keeping the balls at a low bounce. Pick different sections and have them work on getting the balls to move in the right way to best reflect the dynamics.
- The third way you could use the noise meter would be to integrate it into a lesson on the science of sound. Objects move faster when they are louder and higher in pitch. They move more slowly when they are softer and lower in pitch. Bring up the idea of sound waves and how sound travels and have students do some interactive work with their voices or instruments and the sound meter. Ask the questions, "How can you get the balls to be constantly still?" and "How you can get them to be constantly moving?"
- A final suggestion is to use this during a lesson on different voices. You could place a challenge on the students, to make the bouncing balls move a certain way. A whispering voice will cause the balls to move only a bit, if at all. A yelling voice would get the balls to go wild, while a speaking or singing voice would allow them to bounce around at a moderate pace. This tip again can give students a visual on where their voice is. You can discuss before you practice these voices on where best to use them. They certainly do not want to use a yelling voice while in the same room with a sleeping baby; a whispering voice would be better. A speaking voice might not be the

best if an alligator is chasing you, but a yelling voice would undoubtedly be better to get someone's attention.

Assessment Tip: Pick a handful of musical pieces, some loud and some quiet. Play each part with the noise meter on the board. Ask the class to identify whether the music is loud or soft. This activity will demonstrate learned knowledge of dynamics using their aural skills.

Audience Sing-Along

Recommended Grades: K–9
    Difficulty: Moderate
    Time: 30 min.–1 hr. 30 min.
    Objective: Students will perform as an ensemble with their peers and school faculty.

Resources

- Computer
- Projector
- PowerPoint
- Speakers
- Holiday MP3s (I purchased mine from iTunes, so I would always have them)
- Audacity (Only if you want to edit the MP3s for the show such as lowering the volume of the vocals or slowing down the tempo.)

In my first year of teaching, I was so excited to put on a winter concert. Then I found out the school where I was teaching did not usually have a winter show. But they did have an assembly right before school let out where our amazing principal would read Clement C. Moore's classic poem, "'Twas the Night Before Christmas." With the permission of the principal, I took it upon myself to add music again to their holiday assembly. To do that with the least amount of pressure, I created several PowerPoints with classic holiday tunes and the music to go along with them. Some of these songs had to be edited. Using the Audacity audio editing software, I could lower the volume of the voice in the recording so everyone could still hear it but sing along, or I could slow down the music, or even take out entire verses if needed. Once I had a PowerPoint with several sets of song lyrics in it, I put a playlist together of all the music. I could play it in a separate iTunes playlist in the background or I could play it through a different audio channel through an iPad or a smartphone. I chose the iTunes playlist route because it was easier for me, but you could have a separate device plugged in if that is easier for you. I was then able to use the last couple of classes before the holiday break to practice the songs with the students. Then we all got together in the gym and had a giant sing-along before the principal read his traditional story and the students merrily went on their way to holiday break.

Before the Sing-Along

- Using PowerPoint or Keynote, create a presentation by copying and pasting the lyrics to your favorite holiday pieces. Add a title slide between each piece as a buffer. You could use a site like lyrics.com to find all of the words. Using pictures and clip art, you can add a little pizazz to your lyrics PowerPoint.
- You can upload MP3s to presentations to put directly on the slides, but I suggest playing them separately to avoid having playback issues during performance time. You will be unable to play the same song over multiple lyrics screens if you embed it on the first slide itself so embedding on the page will only work if all of the lyrics are on one slide. Play it on a music playlist on your computer or have a separate audio channel to play music through an iPhone or iPod as you operate the slide show.
- There are many inexpensive karaoke MP3s available on iTunes, which make for perfect accompaniment tracks, so you can focus on the kids and fun rather than trying to do that and play accompaniment at the same time. If you need to adjust the audio for these tracks, download Audacity (https://www.audacityteam.org/download/) and use that to make edits to your tracks.
  - You can slow down the track by selecting the whole song, then clicking Effect and Change Tempo.
  - If you want to cut out part of a clip entirely, select the region that you want to get rid of and click on the Scissors icon to trim it.
  - If you would like to remove the vocals from a track, on the left side click the down arrow and click Split Stereo Track. Select the vocals track, click Effect and then click Invert. Then select the downward arrow on both the upper and lower tracks and click on Mono.
  - If you would like to lower the volume of the vocals on a track, on the left side, click the down arrow and click Split Stereo Track. Select the vocals track, click Amplify, and adjust the volume softer until it is to your preference.
- You can put your playlist together in iTunes to play straight from your computer, which would be easiest to control during the performance. You could also put your playlist on your iPhone or iPad or burn it to a CD. Do whatever will play best with your music system.
- If you have time, prepare your students to sing the pieces. Sing through them together as a group a class period or two before. This activity brings the classes together during the fun but stressful time of the holiday season. The first year I did this, I had each grade level practice one particular song along and prepare a couple of group songs. It made it easier for them to remember, and they felt special standing up during the assembly to share.
- Wherever you are going to have the sing-along, make sure you have the proper technology available. If you are in a gym area or cafeteria, I suggest making sure you have access to a sound system to play the music and someone to press Play. A solid projection screen with a projector cart will be needed as well. You can connect your computer

to the system directly to project the lyrics. Luckily you do not need the Internet to make this work!

- On the day of the sing-along, set and check the tech before you start! If you can, do it in the morning or the night before. Set it up and test it out beforehand to make sure it all works. You will need to make sure all of the PowerPoint slides go forward as expected, and the speakers are the perfect sound level for everyone to hear. (Tip: If you want to check the levels, walk to the four corners of the performance space as well as the center of it and make sure you can hear well in each place.)

- When all students are ready, use your presentation with the lyrics as an attention-getter. Have a slide to draw them in and quiet down before starting, maybe a funny snowman video or a slide that has a picture of an audience sitting down waiting to start. In our case it was just an hour or two before the winter break and students were understandably excited and ready to party, so it was important to set a quieter tone so they could pay attention.

- We played our songs back-to-back to save time for everything else we wanted to do in the assembly. There was no talking between songs. Even when I had separate grades stand up to do their unique songs, we were quick and quiet about it to keep students engaged and attentive to what was happening. You can certainly choose to speak between songs, or you might use lyric slides for a concert. Just remember to have someone there to start and stop your playlist at the right times if you are speaking between songs.

- Make sure to have a volunteer sit at the computer to click the slides. This could be another staff member, or even an older student you trust with the computer and music system. If you are unable to find a volunteer, another option is timing the slides, which is an option under the Slideshow menu. Timing slides has to be very precise, or the PowerPoint can get out of sync with the track, so take your time with it.

- Make sure to have lots of fun! This activity is a community builder and a great way to come together as a school during holiday times! Get dressed up. Have the teachers do a fun song together for the students. Get a little silly. It's the holidays, after all!

Assessment Tip: Assess students on their concert etiquette during the sing-along.

Watching YouTube Clips

Recommended Grades: K–12
   Difficulty: Beginner
   Time: 5 min.–1 hr.
   Objective: Students will discover more about other musical cultures and experiences in the world around them through video visuals.

Resources

- Computer with Internet access
- Projector
- Speakers
- YouTube

YouTube is the best place to find engaging visuals, from full orchestras playing well known classical pieces, to short demos of proper singing techniques. I have many lists of videos for every occasion. They are not something that I play every day, but they are great for driving a point home or taking a movement break. It is also a great way to bring a little of the outside world to my students that they might not be able to experience in real life. If I cannot bring flamenco dancers to my classroom, I certainly would be able to find a video for students to see! It is also a beautiful place to create video playlists for any topic that I want to show in class. It could be anything from movement videos, to songs that are demonstrating certain chord progressions. I share these playlists with colleagues or put them on my desktop as shortcuts and instruct substitutes to click on certain ones as part of my sub tote. I have three main playlists: one for movement breaks, one for classical pieces, and one for regular videos or story videos that I easily integrate into lessons.

Before Class

- Plan out your videos beforehand and put them into playlists. Do not search for a video during class time. You never know what might happen when you type in specific search terms for videos with a class of students watching your every move.
  - A suggestion for a couple of starter playlists could be
    - Classical music
    - Animated stories
    - Dance videos
    - Visual examples for a lesson
- Use the playlists tool to your advantage. Create an account and then use the Add button to select the videos you would like to keep. Make sure you separate the videos into playlists you will remember. After a while, your collection can get quite big! You can easily create a new playlist by clicking Create New in that Add area. Then you can access your lists from the left-hand side every time you go to YouTube and are logged in. If you need a specific video, you can use the URL from the Share area of the video page and copy and paste that into any lesson plan, PowerPoint, or folder where you store your lesson resources.
- On the day of class, make sure your video is going to play all the way through. Play it once before your students arrive and then leave that tab up for your lesson. Even if you have fast Wi-Fi, the video will play better if you load it beforehand.

- Make sure that you have the video cued up to the place where you want it to start playing and that you have already watched through any ads that might play before the video begins.
- If your district has any issues with YouTube, try to pick the videos out beforehand and use a safe video app such as SafeShare.TV to create downloadable versions of the videos you can use later. You need the YouTube URL of the video that you would like, and then all you have to do is paste the URL into space on the website and click the arrow to create a video that is free from ads and suggested videos. With a free SafeShare account, you can store up to twenty videos.

During Class

- A great way to use YouTube clips is to show examples of ensembles playing. You cannot always bring a jazz ensemble or have an orchestra come to play in person for your students, but you can still show them a video clip. You can also find clips if you are teaching a unit on instruments. You can show the students examples of how each instrument sounds.
- There is a whole genre of video on YouTube and other sites called the virtual or digital field trip, a way to take students on trips to every corner of the planet without ever leaving their seats. It is a great way to show them different cultures, musical genres, and movers and shakers in music. You can always choose different lengths of trips, from 5 minutes to an hour, depending on what others have created in your subject. Can't find the right video? How about making one on your next summer adventure that your new crop of students will be able to enjoy for the next school year!

Assessment Tip: Two suggestions in regards to assessment ideas for this activity:

- Show students a video clip of the concept you are teaching and ask comprehension questions about what they saw. Assess the class's understanding of the idea by how they answer the questions.
- Another option would be to give students the mission to find a video clip that is an excellent example of the concept you are teaching. Whether it's an orchestra playing a specific piece that demonstrates a particular theory concept or music from a particular culture, have students present it to the class (after you have approved the clip) and give a short explanation as to why it is an excellent example for the concept. Assess them on their choices and interpretations.

Introduction to the Drum Set

Recommended Grades: 1–4
   Difficulty: Moderate
   Time: 10–30 min.

Objective: Students will demonstrate knowledge of basic and advanced rhythms through playing instruments.

Resources

- Computer
- Projector
- Speakers
- Wireless mouse
- Rhythm sticks
- Drumbit.app

I find with my older students that when they are drumming in my class they are the happiest. I have students who love music, but only the music that they listen to on their own, and not what we do in class. So I try to be sensitive to their likes and bring in aspects of that music to their lessons, which makes them more engaged. I am lucky enough to have a majority of students who are heavily into classic rock—from the Stones to the Beatles, they are hooked on it all. I wanted to do something memorable with a particular fifth grade class toward the end of one of my first years of teaching. I had a whole bucket of rhythm sticks that were waiting to be used. We practiced our rock beat for a bit before I brought up one of the popular songs of the time. Their faces lit up, and they quietly listened as I brought up the rhythm on the board and played the beat before having them join in with me. They started singing along and playing the song together. Sticks were flying, and teachers were coming in to watch the commotion with smiles on their faces. It was a memorable time for them as they were making music in class that related to the music they listened to outside of the school day. At one point I had the class pause and I began playing the two lines at once as the class listened intently. After a minute, one of my "chair drummers" shouted out, "Hey! That's a rock beat on the drum set!" I nodded my head with a grin and mouthed "try it." They were ecstatic as I listened to the sweet sound of floor drumming for a good 10 minutes. The students were engaged because it was a teachable skill they could master quickly, to emulate their favorite rock stars. As students were leaving, they could not stop talking about how it was the best music class they'd ever had.

Before Class

- Double-check Internet connection to make sure everything is running quickly.
  - If you suspect your Internet might be having an issue, head to https://fast.com, and do an Internet speed test. The more Mbps you have, the better. If you have anything under 6 Mbps, then it is time to contact your technology department to have your Internet connection checked out.
- Make sure the tools you want to use are compatible with your school computer. This trick means that you need to test it on the machine you will be using for a class before you try it with students.

- Make sure the sound works on your machine and is loud enough that the students can hear it when everyone is playing. It will get quite noisy when you start bringing in rhythm sticks and vocal ostinatos.
- Make sure you have enough rhythm sticks (or drumsticks) for the class plus a few extras in case of breakage.
- On the day of class, bring up the tool that you are going to use on your computer, so you have it ready.
- Test it out to make sure that it is still working for the class.
- Get the rhythm sticks out.

During Class

- This activity is great to introduce students to the straightforward rock beat that you can play on a drum set. It would also be an excellent introduction to a bucket drumming unit, or you can use this as an activity during a more general lesson. You do not necessarily need to do this beat; you can always create and perform other rhythms, but it is a recognizable one for many.
  - First, all you will need the high hat and snare lines that you will do with students in the Drumbit.app. Before the activity starts, put a steady beat in the kick line. The other lines you will do with the class in front of you.
  - When students come in, have the activity up and have them sit in their regular seats. Play the bass line and have them stomp every time the kick hits on the beat. (You could also practice the beat using their voices with the word "Boom" acting like a bass drum. Practice saying "Boom" together as a class every time the kick drum plays.)
  - When students have the bass mastered. Add the high-hat line. Have students practice the motion of playing the high hat while still stomping their feet to the kick drum. (If you need to simplify the activity you can have one half of the group keep repeating the word "Boom" to the kick drum line and then have the other half say "Ticka-Ticka" for the high-hat line.)
  - Next, when they had both parts in, add the snare line and have them practice the motions for all three lines. (A simplified version of this would be to divide the class into three groups and have the bass line group say "Boom," the high-hat group say "Ticka Ticka," and the snare group say "Tah." Making sure to rotate the groups around, so each group gets to experience each part.)
  - When students are ready, pass out drumsticks or rhythm sticks and have all students sit in a horseshoe shape so all can see the board. Practice each line saying and playing.
  - Then divide up the class again; each group plays the high hat, bass, and snare lines together, and then switches parts, so everyone has a turn playing each line.

o When they are ready, have students put all three parts together. See if they can tell what kind of beat they are playing.

o Put on a song in the rock genre and have students play along using the beat they just learned. Put a few different songs on so they can get a feel for how the beat carries over into pieces of music.

Assessment Tip: Use this as a performance-based assessment. Wander around the room and spend a few moments with each student as they play along with the class. Assess them on how they are keeping up with the ensemble and performing the rhythms for the song.

Composing

Recommended Grades: 2–7

Difficulty: Moderate

Time: 10–30 min.

Objective: Students will demonstrate mastery of basic music theory taught in class by using compositional software to create a short piece of music.

Resources
- Computer
- Projector
- Speakers
- *Wireless mouse
- Website—Noteflight.com or Finale.com (download their Notepad software for free!)

In my early years of teaching, we did a lot of composing using different music composition tools. I didn't have an interactive board in my room, so I had to figure out other ways to make it engaging. We usually compose pieces as a whole class, and I sometimes use these times to assess my students on different theoretical aspects we are learning. Having students learn the names of the notes and rests to tell you what to put on the staff, or tell you where on the staff to place it, can indicate how much knowledge the students are retaining. Then you can work on critical thinking skills by playing the piece and have them edit it together! In my first year of teaching, I partnered up with a friend of mine who was in a different district, also teaching elementary music. My class and I used Finale Notepad together and composed a phrase. We then came up with one question to ask one of my friend's classes, then sent off the phrase and the question to him. He did the same thing with his classes and sent us back their added phrase and inquiry along with their answer to our question. We went back and forth until we created a full piece and got to know more about another class from a different city in our state. Later, we were able to share the work with our administration and school communities to show what we had done. If we wanted to go further, we could have video chatted afterward to meet each other.

Before Class

- Some compositional tools require an account or paid license. Know the tools you are going to be working with and make sure that you either have an account set up or the program downloaded and working correctly. This is something you can do at the beginning of the year and never have to worry about it again. If you want to have a more advanced license, you will need to purchase the software. Noteflight Premium and the full version of Finale have more features like unlimited scores, more editing tools, and sharing platforms. You might need to put in a request to your school purchasing agent. Most software suppliers now do take POs as well as standard payment methods.
- Also, make sure your speakers are in top shape to hear the compositions that your students make. This allows you to play back what you compose, including the dynamic markings.
- Acquire one or two beach balls and write a bunch of notes and rests on them.
- On the day of class, make sure the program is loaded, the Internet is working properly if needed, and the speakers are operating normally.

During Class

- Having only a projector doesn't mean that you can't make an activity interactive. Acquire a wireless mouse from your local office supply store and put it on a stool or table at the front of the room. To play this game, start with a short phrase and have each student come up, and they can add either one note or one rest to the music. The trick is, they can only fill up one measure at a time, so they cannot add to the next measure until the one before it is filled. Have each student come up to take a turn at the mouse until everyone has had a turn. Listen to the finished piece and have students volunteer to come up and make edits where they think the piece of music needs it.
  - Another variation of this would be to have students come up to the board and ask them to tell you what kind of note or rest they want to add in, and the measure and beat they want to put it in. This activity helps students practice naming notes and rests as well as staff placement and naming beats of a measure.
  - Have the students listen to a piece of music, and then together try to follow the melodic contour of the music as best they can by drawing it. Later, play the piece they drew alongside the other part. Have them listen to see how it sounds and explain how they have created another layer to the existing section. Suggested pieces of music include:
    - "Ode to Joy"
    - *Carmen* Overture
    - "In the Hall of the Mountain King"
    - *Eine Kleine Nachtmusik*
    - *Appalachian Spring*

- Here is an activity for center time. Have each group build a 2- to 4-measure composition during their allotted time and then have the whole class listen to what they created together. Directions for this could be as follows:
  - Work together as a group to complete a 4-measure melody with the following characteristics:
    - Smooth melodic contour that moves up and down the staff.
    - At least three different types of notes and one type of rest that you have learned.
    - Tempo marking of your own choosing.
    - Dynamic marking of your own choosing.
      Save your music as your team name to the desktop of the computer so it can be played later for the class!
- Find a fellow music teacher in another district, school, or state to be your class's "pen pal." This activity has become easier with the power of social media. Head into a music teacher's group on Facebook or participate in a chat on Twitter to find new colleagues from all over the globe. Have your class compose a line of music together and then send it to their pen pal class. That group of students should add another line to it and send it back. Send the piece back and forth until the music is complete. Then have each class record themselves playing music together and send it to their pen pals for viewing! If you want to go a little further, try to edit the two videos together to make one big performance!
  - Note: This could be followed up by a video chat between the two classes to "meet" each other virtually. Even if they are only a few towns away, their lives could be different. Have each class come up with a few questions for each other about their daily lives to learn more about the experiences of students in a different part of the state, country, or even the world.
  - A variation on this for older students could be to set them up with individual pen pals. Students can video chat or email with their pen pal to plan their piece first, then start the process of writing their phrases back and forth to each other. If you are using cloud-based software, you can have them set up a single account under the same login for this activity or use software such as Soundation where they can collaborate in real time. If they are using downloadable composing software, then have the students save the file to their file storage database or desktop and then email it to their pen pal, who will do the same. If you have the time in this project, you can have your students do a halfway-point check-in with each other to talk about and edit the piece so far. Have them add a tempo and a dynamic marking as well. When they are done with their work, then they can present it to their respective classes. Then have them video chat one last time to wrap up, discuss, and reflect on the process to the final product.
- Put your composition software up on the board. You will need either one, two, or three lines on the staff depending on the level of the class. An example would be one line for kindergarten and first-grade students, two lines for your second- and third-grade classes,

and three lines for fourth- and fifth-grade classes. Each line would be a separate rhythmic ostinato part so you can divide your class into different groups to play each part.

o Start bopping the beach balls around the class like popcorn. Start counting down 3 . . . 2 . . . 1 . . . DONE—whoever has the balls must hold them and tell you what note or rest is under their right hands. Have a few practice rounds before you start writing it down. Try to have the ball land on different people each time.

o When you have your ostinatos, pass out instruments and assign parts. I tried to have at least one strong rhythmic student on each part and coaxed the other members in the same group to watch that person to keep the beat because it was challenging to play three parts at once.

o Practice each part as a class before you start putting them together. My students knew when I said "Ostinato" to keep repeating until I played a finishing drum sound or gave a vocal cue.

Assessment Tip: Using the digital compositions created by your students, assess their knowledge of basic music theory. You can have them export their pieces as printed sheet music to submit to you for grading later.

Movement Break

Recommended Grades: 2–8
Difficulty: Beginner
Time: 5–15 min.
Objective: The class will demonstrate proficiency in feeling the beat and working memory skills by moving to choreographed dances.

Resources
- Computer
- Projector
- Speakers
- YouTube playlist (Here's mine: https://youtu.be/ycq_E6sN3CI)

My students beg every class for a chance to be able to do one of the many movement breaks I have in a YouTube playlist. Of course, we do a lot of moving, playing, singing, and shaking in my room, but they can't get enough of these movement break videos. They are also fantastic to leave for a sub! The videos are shorter in length and give students basic and repetitive dance moves to that can be learned quickly. There are many days, especially the ones before a school break, where I have two or three fun favorite videos ready to go just in case there is a rowdy crowd of kids prepared for a quick dance party, but it wasn't yet time to leave for the holiday. I also make sure they have worked on essential movement concepts in the curriculum such as moving to the beat, crossing the midline, and moving more than one body part at the same time.

Before Class

- Create a playlist of your favorite movement breaks on YouTube. You can do this by
  - Creating your own YouTube account.
  - Searching for the videos you would like and click on the Share button. You can also click the Create New Playlist button and start a new playlist for your videos.
  - Continuing to add videos to your playlist.
- Go through your list and tag each of the videos with the concept it works best with. For example, the floss dance helps students practice moving two body parts at the same time. The lawnmower dance provides practice going across the midline. Any dance club or rap music encourages keeping a steady beat.
- Practice some of the more involved dances yourself so you can teach them to students piece-by-piece before they do the whole dance with the video.
- Before each class, make sure you have a reliable Internet connection, and your videos are correctly loaded.
- Choose one or two options that go along with the lesson; that way, students get to experience the fun while applying those skills they learned from the current lesson.

During Class

- For this activity, you can partner up with your physical education teacher to have students gain even more experience and knowledge from this adventure.
  - Together, choose a grade level and a dance song that the two of you feel would not only be appropriate for the grade level but will also teach students different concepts that overlap in both of your curricula. For example, both music and PE classes might be working on moving to a steady beat or keeping the pace.
  - In your respective classrooms, work on activities that help practice each of those goals. Your colleague might have some exercises that will help the students while you might have them move to simple marches or work on drumming techniques.
  - While this is happening, start working on different movements broken down into bite-sized chunks. Work with your colleague to practice the same moves at the same time or work on different steps that play to your strengths.
  - When students have learned the different parts of the dance song, put it all together and start practicing with the video playing on the screen using the projector.
  - This activity can be part of a concert, an assembly flash mob, or even an "informance" with a couple of teachers and administrators. Have the students show off what they have been learning together and how far they have come! If

you perform in a bigger space, get a projector cart and run the video through a projector, then run the audio through the speakers in the area or a set of higher quality computer speakers.

- Use this activity as an incentive, or when you have a video that relates to your instruction. Bring up the clip, get your students ready, turn up the speakers, and click Play!
- Use your playlist for sub plans. Leave them a few specific videos to play with the students while you are out.
  - o Directions for the substitute:
    - ▪ "I have a playlist of dance videos set up that you can use during the last 10 minutes of class.
    - ▪ Turn on the projector.
    - ▪ Open Google Chrome.
    - ▪ Click on My Favorites and select Substitute Video Playlist.
    - ▪ You can have students select songs only from the playlist. They are not allowed to pick anything that is not on that list. If they become too out of control, please stop the activity and go back to read another book or worksheet that I left. Ten minutes should get you about three video choices."

Assessment Tip: Observe and assess students as they put the beat into their bodies and demonstrate working memory skills by remembering the choreography.

Concert Performance Video Playback

Recommended Grades: 2–12
Difficulty: Beginner
Time: 15 min.–2 hrs.
Objective: Students will demonstrate thoughtful reflections on their performance by watching a video playback of their work and discussing it.

Resources
- Computer
- Projector
- Speakers
- Video of the concert performance
- Whiteboard and markers

This activity is one of the simplest things you can do with your projector. I do this with my choirs; it's one of the things my students always look forward to. I have the concert recording ready along with a snack and we sit and watch their performance together before reflecting on how they did. I usually do a little bit of fancy editing using iMovie before we spend the class period watching the show. After the show is over, we typically take turns creating a wall of written positive thoughts about the performance, making sure each student gets a turn. I then have a large colorful wall of reflections and positivity and I take a photo collage of everything to keep. My choirs love this time and look forward to doing it after each concert. I work at two schools during the year and have built up their two programs back from near-extinction, and these groups have grown to significant size. We call it an end-of-year "party," where we have snacks, watch the concert, and have a great time. It brings a lot of students together.

FIGURE 3.2 An example of a reflection wall. My students have so much fun with these! (Photo Credit C. Dwinal)

Before Class

• I usually recruit a family member to video our shows for me. You could get a family member or even a student's parent to do it for you. You do not necessarily need an actual camera to record it. Using a phone will usually provide a great movie. After you get the video file from the appointed videographer, make sure to watch it all the way through and do any editing if necessary. You never know if a random thumb or a camera drop might make an appearance halfway through the performance! I usually make a fancy title slide like curtains opening with the title of the concert, then I put all of the student's names in the closing credits. They always love to see their names on the "big screen"!

- If you feel like going a little above and beyond, get some snacks ahead of time. My first time doing this, I bought a couple of packs of snack popcorn packs and juice boxes. After a while, choir parents joined the effort and now go all-out with the snacks, and we have a great party!
- If necessary, borrow some more whiteboard markers from your fellow teachers for this activity. You should have plenty of room for students to create a wall of reflection.
- On the day of class, test your speakers to make sure that they will be loud enough for the video. Also, test out the actual video to make sure the whole thing will play through. (If you edited it, make sure to export it as a movie to your desktop to get the best playback. It will usually play out of video players like QuickTime or iTunes after exporting.)
- Set out markers for the wall and snacks if you want to have them! If you do not have a big enough whiteboard, you can always get some art paper and place it on the floor or a table. Grab some regular markers or crayons and have students make a paper version instead!

During Class

- Once everyone is comfy, dim the lights for a theater experience.
  - During the video, you can have students quietly reflect in a few different ways:
    - Have students think of one thing that went well about the concert and one thing they see that they could have done better. Encourage them to write and draw pictures on the board!
    - Create a worksheet to guide them through the reflection process. This worksheet can have individual thought starters for students to better reflect on their performance. Things that it could include:
- Notes on stage presence. Were they distracted or distracting to their classmates? Were they safe on stage? Did they follow directions?
- Did they sing their best? Did they use proper singing posture when they were on stage?
- How did they sound as a group? Have students provide some full ensemble feedback that gives a little more detail than words like "good" or "meh." Have them write a few sentences about the overall group performance.
    - Suggest music for the next concert! Have students give (within reason!) suggestions on music for next season or a new theme for the upcoming concert. It's an excellent way for them to feel connected and have a little bit of ownership over the show they will be putting on for next time.
  - Make sure to bring the students back together after the video for a full class review and discussion about how the concert went overall. This review will be an excellent closer before they leave.

Assessment Tip: Assess students on the content of their written reflections.

Skype

Recommended Grades: 2–12
Difficulty: Moderate
Time: 30 min.–1 hr. 30 min.
Objective: Students will perform for their peers via video chat services.

Resources
- Computer with Internet access
- Projector
- Webcam
- https://education.skype.com

I work in a small school system in the middle of a place where half the kids might not ever leave the state. Showing students that there is a world outside of their familiar surroundings by using just a projector and a web camera creates lasting memories. The first time I ever did a Skype call, I remember having the entire fourth grade class come in. The students we were communicating with were doing a Skype sleepover sing-along, and we were their U.S. stopover. The room was abuzz with excitement. The students were the most well behaved they had ever been as we Skyped with the school in England. I had our tech coordinator come in and watch, and made sure to get plenty of pictures and videos. The students we were chatting with sang a few songs that they had been practicing, and my students sang "Yankee Doodle" and "Grand Old Flag" to demonstrate some music from our country. Afterward, when everyone was gone, I sent a video of what we did to the rest of the fourth-grade teachers and the principal so they could see what an excellent experience the students had. The principal came up to me a month or so later in the lunchroom during duty. "I was sitting with some of the kids. Did you know they're still talking about how cool that Skype call was?" It was special to create an experience the students remembered for a long time. Allowing them to speak with someone like them but from a different culture across the ocean was something that was an engaging experience.

Before the Call
- Before you get started, you need to make sure that your systems are in complete working order. Check that your computer is updated, make sure that the Skype program has been downloaded and is operational, check to make sure that your projector is working, and also make sure that your webcam is placed in the best area for the students to show their beautiful faces.
- Go to Microsoft's Skype in the Classroom website. This website allows you to create an account and customized profile that will let other teachers across the globe connect with you to set up Skype calls. Make sure that inside your profile, you explicitly state what kinds of Skype calls you are looking to do. Types of calls can range from

FIGURE 3.3 Here we are sharing a song we have been learning with another class on video chat (Photo Credit C. Dwinal)

performances to Mystery Skypes to whatever you can dream up. Be specific in what you would like.

- Once you create an account on the Skype website, start looking in the community for other teachers like you looking for Skype calls.
- You can message other teachers to introduce yourself and set up call times right on the website.
- Make sure to do a test call with your collaborative teacher either a day or two before or the morning of to make sure everything is going to work correctly. It might have worked a week ago, but due to computer updates and Wi-Fi bandwidth issues, there might be trouble making a connection. That's why you need to do a test call; if something is not going to plan, you have time to get one of your loyal technology specialists to get it working for you!
- Generally, with a music class, you probably will be doing some Skype performance or song sharing time. Prepare one or two songs that students will be able to perform for your visitors on the other end of the call.
- Once you have set up a call or two, prepare your students for what is going to happen. They might need to come to music class at a different time, or there needs to be a new

set of rules place down for when they enter the room. Here are some rules that I set with my students whenever we had a video chat with another class:

- You represent your school, your teachers, and yourselves. Be on your best behavior!
- Do not get discouraged by any technology interruptions. If something goes wrong, go with the flow.
- Stay quiet! You will get a chance to sing for them and ask your questions as long as you do not purposely interrupt the chat. The microphone picks up all sounds, and we can't talk to them if the microphone is busy!
- Be respectful; our friends might have a different culture than ours.
- Be willing to learn about others! You get a chance to talk to someone like you that is in a different part of the world. Listen! Learn!
- On the day of the call, set up the room where all students will fit in the frame (you might need risers, or chairs and a rug).
- Test your connection beforehand with the other teacher to make sure everything works. It might be the day before, or in the morning during your prep time.
- When students come in, keep a calm and quiet environment to get them settled and focused. Your Skype partners will hear every word and movement, and see most of what is happening in the room. Set a high standard from the beginning.
- A song share is when one group talks and sings while the other listens, and then they switch. A Skype performance usually is one-sided, with one group acting as the audience and the other performing, like a typical concert.
- Remember, during the Skype call:
  - Make sure to ask the other group where they are Skyping from! Have the students prepare a few questions to ask.
  - Have background information on your songs, especially if you were in a case like mine when we were Skyping with a class across the ocean that had never heard our patriotic pieces.
  - Be patient with students taking time to say hello. If you want to go further after your call, turn this into a pen pal project you can work on with their classroom teachers!
- After the call, make sure to send thanks to your teacher counterpart and stay in touch. The more calls and friends you make, the easier it is to have even more students connect.

Variation:
- Set up a Mystery Skype with another ensemble. A Mystery Skype is a type of video chat where each class of students needs to work together to figure out where the other is by asking questions and doing research. They cannot reveal to each other their exact location until the end, when the final guess takes place! You can make this musical by having students share their favorite genres of music, concerts they

have seen, folk songs from their area of the world, and their favorite artists. There are all kinds of resources set up through Skype Education and through social media venues such as Twitter and Facebook that give more detailed instructions on how to set up a Mystery Skype. Here is an official page from Microsoft that talks about the game and lists some great starter resources: https://education.microsoft.com/skype-in-the-classroom/mystery-skype

Assessment Tip: Have students write a short reflection on their experience. This activity can be done using anything from pencil and paper to Google Docs. Assess students on the content of their observations. Alternatively, you can have the students participate in a class discussion to reflect on their experience.

Projecting Music to Play

Recommended Grades: 2–12
Difficulty: Beginner
Time: 5 min.–1 hr.
Objective: Students will practice looking up from their music stand by playing music projected on the board.

Resources
- Computer
- Projector
- PDFs of scores or lyrics sheets.

Projecting music on the board for all to see is such a simple way for any music educator to start using technology. It is a substitution that not only saves trees but also gets students practicing to look up beyond their music stands and pay attention to the conductor! Of course, this isn't ideal for every piece of music but it is excellent for simple songs and exercises, especially in general music class or during warm-ups and sight-reading for larger ensembles! I did this all the time when I first started; I took all of the old scores I saved from college and ones that my predecessor had left me that were copyright-free and scanned them onto my computer and organized them in a big folder. When I began to use QuaverMusic in my classroom, it became even more accessible, and the scores were even more engaging for students because of all the animations and highlighting. The best use for this in my class is when it is time for recorders. I do Recorder Karate with a mix of Quaver songs. Groups earn belts based on how they play together and what I can tell from their practicing. I can easily pop up whatever piece the class is working on so we can practice it together as a group. The music is large enough for everyone to see from anywhere in the room.

Before Class

- Find the music you would like to project on to the board. You might have boxes of music that were left over from a previous teacher, or use your own ever-growing collection. Pick out what you are going to use before scanning.
- Make sure you have all of your music that you would like to project in a digital format. You might need to scan any originals on paper into a PDF format. Place everything into a secure access folder. (You might be concerned about copyright infringement, but as long as the material is not used for performances, for monetary gain, or passed out for students to keep, it is fair use. Also, make sure that you keep any paper copies of the music somewhere safe.)
- If you want to create exercises and sight-reading pieces, use a notation software such as Finale to compose what you would like and save it. This way, you can save it as a PDF and put it directly to a folder.
- Make sure your scores or exercises are pulled up before each class, and are working so that students can correctly see them. (If you have any animated scores that require Wi-Fi, make sure to play them to verify that the Internet is working at a reasonable speed.)

During Class

- Have a full piece of music on the board for everyone to see. This activity is beneficial for a general music classroom. There are programs out there such as QuaverMusic. com that have full scores for hundreds of songs that highlight and paginate themselves. Make sure everything is up on one page so you won't have to do any zooming or scrolling. Or you can divide it up into different parts and only practice a couple of lines of music at a time.
  o Find a piece of music that you want to work on during the lesson, bring it up during the students' practice time and use it as your visual. It is a simple alternative to copying and passing out a massive stack of sheet music or playing with the chance of losing their attention as you write the exercises on the board for the class.
- The other way is to have exercises and sight-reading on the board at the start of rehearsals as warm-ups. When I was teaching choir, we warmed up at the beginning of every rehearsal. Most days they sang memorized warm-ups while I played the piano or used a warm-up track. When I wanted to teach them a new warm-up or do a little sight-reading, I would put the exercise up on the board for everyone to learn and read along.

Assessment Tip: Give students the printed music as well as projecting it on the board. Have a contest: the person who looks up from their music stand the most to see the board wins.

Webquests

Recommended Grades: 2–12
Difficulty: Expert
Time: 10–55 min.
Objective: Students will practice independent learning and knowledge of learned subjects through the completion of the assigned webquest.

Resources

- Projector
- Computer
- Google Docs or Microsoft Word
- Individual devices
- List of websites that students will be visiting.

A webquest is a series of directions instructing students around a website or series of sites to help them find information on a specific topic, which could be anything from composers to fundamental theory. Each quest has a particular objective, puzzle to solve, or question to answer, and a final product a student creates, so it can be a tremendous final assessment for a unit or even a portfolio artifact. I put all the instructions on the board for students to see during their quest. Sometimes I ask them to write the final answer on the board (if it is a puzzle) or write a symbol on the board that represents the hidden meaning of the quest if they get it before we pull together for closing circle. I love doing webquests with my students. My students love being given a set of directions and then set free. I always have a few waiting in the wings for a day where students need some peace, or right before a break when students want to do something a little different than the normal "It is almost holiday time" activities. I created an eBook with all of the webquests related to a specific website such as QuaverMusic.

Before Class

- Rent out individual devices for students to use for this activity or if you are a 1:1 device school, make sure they bring their devices to class for this lesson.
- Choose the websites you will use for this activity. If you are looking for suggestions, check out the resource guide at the end of this book. Make sure that you check each website as well to make sure that they are operable on your school network.
- Write out the webquest directions into a document to pass out to students; or alternately, you could customize them into a PowerPoint slide to project on to the board. Make the instructions clear and concise.
- On the day of class, check the websites that you plan to use. Make sure they are operable on the student devices.

FIGURE 3.4 A class deep into another webquest (Photo Credit C. Dwinal)

- If you feel like you need some assistance, do not be afraid to ask a member of the tech department to sit in on the class and help out if needed.
- Bring up the instructions on the board and make sure students can see from all corners of the room.

During Class

- Post the instructions on the board so all can see them.
  - Explain to the students that they will be working independently. They will need to follow the directions on the board (or in the document you passed out) to navigate around the websites to meet the final goal.
  - Read the directions together and answer questions about the quest.
  - Have students come up in small groups to get their devices out and find a comfy spot in the room where they can work on their quests.
  - Give them plenty of time to create and solve the webquests.
  - If they are required to answer a question on the whiteboard, get markers to write their answers on the board.

- Some examples of final webquest products that they can create for portfolios are:
  - Videos of themselves singing a song from one of the websites they visited.
  - Screen captures of scores of the games that they completed.
  - Exported MP3s or videos of masterpieces they have created from sites they visited.
  - A short paragraph answering a question asked by the webquest.
  - A short reflection paragraph talking about what they learned and discovered on their quest.
- Some examples of questions that students could answer as a final question:
  - Name the piece that Tchaikovsky was best known for.
  - What instrument family did the clavichord come from?
  - How does an object create sound?

The following are some other examples of quests.

QuaverMusic.com—Chorus

A choir is a group of people who get together and sing! They use their voices as instruments. Did you know there are four different types of voices in a choir? Soprano, Alto, Tenor, and Bass. Follow the steps to discover what a choir is all about!

1. Head into the shop, but do not worry! You are not there to purchase anything. Click on the jukebox near the guitars in the window and try to find a song that has more than one person singing in it! Do their voices sound the same or different?
2. Madrigals were written hundreds of years ago in the Renaissance and early Baroque periods and were composed to be performed without any instruments; they were just for the singers! They had many voices singing different parts all at the same time. Head to the Phonebox and travel to the madrigal period to read the book and answer the questions!
3. Usually, choirs sing more than one note at the same time. Do you know that we can call that a chord? Head to the Ear IQ carnival in the lab to test your listening skills in the chord game! Try to listen to each voice!
4. Now here is your big challenge! Go to QComposer on the stage in the Studio. Using the Chord Builder, build a C to F to G to C chord progression and then listen to your creation and try to hear each note as it plays. Then find and place a C to F to G to C phrase in the bass line to add your fourth voice!

Incredibox.com—Loops/Vocal Ostinatos

An ostinato is a short repeated pattern. Can you make your own using Incredibox? Follow the steps below to layer voice ostinatos together and create one rocking tune!

1. Choose one loop from each section and put it together. Try muting a few or soloing one. Can you hear each voice?
2. Now mix it up! Take out at least three of your guys and put in three new ones of your choosing! Do you like how they fit together? If not, what do you need to change?
3. Press the Record button toward the top left of the screen and record it at least halfway through. Then press Share and share your creation with your teacher!

QuaverMusic.com—Dynamics

Dynamics make a piece of music more exciting by allowing it to get LOUD and soft at different times. They add a little spice to turn a simple melody into a killer tune! What do you know about dynamics? Follow the steps around the Quaver world to test your skills!

1. Did you know that the Italian clavichord and harpsichord maker Bartolomeo Cristofori created what we now know as the piano to give musicians an instrument to better play loud and soft? He opened the world of dynamics up to many musicians! Travel back to his time in the Phonebox and read the book and answer the questions to find out more!
2. Next, head to the Jukebox in the Shop and click on the Shop episode songs. Listen to the Use Dynamics track and sing along to learn more about why we use dynamics!
3. Here is the test: Go to the QComposer on the stage in the studio and get out your composing brain! Using only the treble clef line, create a four-measure melody where the dynamics change two times. Try for one loud dynamic marking and one soft. You can change dynamics by clicking the dynamic button on the bottom left and choosing your dynamic, then clicking where you want the level to change in your melody.

QuaverMusic.com—Melodic Contour

Many times, a melody flows smoothly up and down the staff like a river. Sometimes it goes way up and sometimes it goes way down. Float down the river of directions below to learn about how a melody flows.

1. The way a melody moves up and down the staff is called a melodic contour. Head to the painting easel called Songbrush in the Shop and practice making lines that flow up and down across the music staff. Listen to them and hear how the notes go up and down!
2. You will need a piece of paper and a pencil for this one. Now head to the Jukebox and double click Classical Music in the menu. Choose a song and write the title at the top of the page. Now listen to that song and try to draw a line as you did in Songbrush on

the page. Play the song again after you are done and trace the route with your finger. Do you think you followed it?

3. Here's your turn to make your melody that goes up and down like a river on the staff. Go to QComposer and using just the treble clef line create a five-measure melody using only quarter notes that looks smooth, with no big jumps. Save it and play it for a friend to see if they can follow along.

SFSkids.com/Classic—Composing and Creating

It's your turn to be a future famous composer like Bach or Beethoven! Follow the steps to learn how to create a melody yourself.

1. Head to the Compose option up top first; you will stay in this tab for this whole quest! Click on Music Lessons and then The Basics to complete the lesson. You will need this knowledge for later.
2. Head back to the Compose menu and select Starting Tunes, Choose Twinkle Twinkle and listen to the song. Does the song sound incomplete? Finish the last measure.
3. Now head back to the Compose menu one last time and select Quick Start to try your hand at creating a beautiful piece of music!

QuaverMusic.com—Tempo

Tempo can be so tricky! Sometimes a song might go slow, and sometimes it might go fast! Just like a race car! Let's discover how to find tempos as we travel around QuaverMusic.com.

1. You need to turn on your listening ears for this one! Head to the Jukebox in the Shop and find one song that is presto (fast) and one song that is largo (slow.) Write down your findings to share with the group!
2. Head to the Metro and find two different stops that have two different types of tempo. Find a stop that has mostly fast music and one that has primarily slow music.
3. Your challenge is to head to QBackbeat in the Studio and create a beat either Largo, Presto, or Moderato. Then click Play-Along Tracks and select a track at the same tempo. Do both of the tracks fit together?

Assessment Tip: All of the webquests ask students to either share or create a product to demonstrate their knowledge on the specific concept of the webquest. You can assess students based on the products they create and what they share with their classmates.

Animation Clips

Recommended Grades: 3–12
Difficulty: Expert

Time: 5 min.–1 hr.
Objective: Students will demonstrate learned knowledge by creating animated clips.

Resources

- Computer
- Projector
- Speakers
- Powtoon.com
- Individual devices

Imagine a class where students walked in, and to change things up, they are given today's instruction via an animated person. Or they give a presentation on individual composers or musical styles by creating an animation. It's a new way to engage them in the content they are learning and yet still provide them with profound learning experiences that might get them interested in their future profession! You can do activities about found sounds, relate them to science by talking about how Foley artists create old familiar sounds with new materials, and so much more. This is similar to a children's science center that has different stations with different directions and some have interactive screens with all kinds of characters. It holds the students' attention because they are focused on a separate area every few minutes. They do not have to pay attention to one presenter on one topic for more than 5 to 10 minutes at a time. This takes into consideration typical child brain development. We cannot ask a seven-year-old to pay attention to one thing for 15 minutes or more. It is suitable for their stage of learning to break up the instruction. When I teach my lessons, I try to do the same and bring one or two different videos to keep the students' attention during my presentation. Learning is a fluid and ever-changing process; students are not expected to hold their attention for more than a few minutes. Creating another persona through things like cartoons can give you a novel teaching aid that takes a little pressure off you and gives the students something a little different.

Before Class

- If you intend to use an animator as a project for students to create their clips, create an example to show them while you give instructions, so they know the expectations for this project. Develop directions for the activity using the animator. Students can get a fun surprise when hearing the instructions for what they are going to do.
- If you are going to use this as an instructional tool, create and preview your videos before class so you know they are videos you would like to use in your instruction. These videos take a little bit of work on the front end but can be used for a long time afterward. Creating good content for class use takes time! You do not need to rush through this!

- Make sure your video is up and ready to go before each class. If an Internet connection is needed, make sure that it is fully operational before class starts! It would be wise to play through it all the way, to make sure nothing skips during class.

During Class

- If you plan on using these videos as instructional tools (which you can use more than once), create a video that might introduce how to read a rhythm, or detail the life of Mozart. These can be great engaging "hooks" to pull a student into a lesson before starting it. Play it on your computer and over your projector for all students to see.
  - Some examples of videos you can create to be your animated assistants:
    - Create a character that talks to the kids about composers when you are in the middle of your musical history unit. Consider it a "guest" students can look forward to, that gives you a break for to grab a quick swig of coffee or water.
    - Create a series of videos that explain the basics of music theory. Make them smaller chunks and use clips from Powtoons to create a "Bill Nye" style video series that you can assign to students to reinforce concepts you are teaching to students.
    - Use an app like Puppet Pals to reenact a story about a composer or defining moment in a musical style. You can use the puppets and do voice-overs right in the app to tell the story as the puppets act it out. If you want to have even more fun, have someone the students know, like a principal or other teacher, narrate.
    - Another strategy to use is to complete a comprehensive assessment to determine what students are still having trouble with at the end of a unit, identify the areas that they could improve, and create a set of short videos that are about the topic. Then you could either incorporate them into lessons, or post them on a webpage for students to study.
- A different way to use this is to ask students to create animated videos that demonstrate their knowledge of the unit that they have been learning. Give them the requirements, such as having five to ten facts or pieces of understanding of the subject, a completed clip with audio, etc. Have them download it and send it to you. This way, you can put it in a video reel and have students watch each other work to see what their classmates also learned about the subject! This activity would be an excellent time for students to use a creator such as Powtoon.com on their laptops; apps like Puppet Pals would be perfect for tablet devices.

Instructions for this:

- o Time to create a video that shows off your knowledge of the history of rock 'n' roll!
    - Research and collect at least eight facts about the history of rock 'n' roll. Make sure each one is different and detailed.
    - Type out each one into a document in order of how you are going to present them in the video.

- Write a short script that incorporates all of the facts that you found.
- Create your video! Add your special flair.
- Export it or copy a shareable link and email it to me for final viewing!

Assessment Tip: Assess students on the content of the animated clips they created based on how well they incorporated the concept, how the video was put together, the validity of the facts in the video, and any other criteria you would like.

The Green Screen Movie Project

Recommended Grades: 4–12
Difficulty: Expert
Time: 30 min. to 2 or 3 class periods
Objective: Students will demonstrate learned collective knowledge of music theory and composition through composing a full song and performing it for the camera.

Resources
- Computer
- Projector
- Do Ink app
- Green screen backdrop (cloth or paper)
- Properly sourced background images
- iPads with iMovie
- YouTube

There have been a few years where we did different collaborative projects within our specialist team as part of our PLC (professional learning community) experience. These projects were data-driven, so we had to comb through state testing data for all of the grade levels before choosing a specific level and skills that the data showed our students could improve in. For this specific project, we chose fifth grade and made the assessments before moving on to the activities. The specific skills we wanted were writing narratives and using technology for research. We used the projector to project images on the background of the video and also to play the videos back for the class's viewing pleasure. The students learned about the history of dance and choreographed a dance routine in PE, they learned about iMovie and video editing in media, and they wrote music in music class. Then we all worked together to record each one of the performances from the students. We were lucky enough to have a lot of the fifth-grade classes at the same time, so filming and editing went a lot faster because we could do it together. Months later, students couldn't stop talking about this project, not only because it carried over into multiple areas of their school day, but it kept them engaged, and they loved to take control of their learning and do something different!

Before Class

- With a project like this, you need to prepare the students by acquiring a few iPads with iMovie on them and teaching students how to use the iMovie program. They will need to have prior knowledge of this skill to be successful with this activity.
- Collaborate with your colleagues to plan out this unit. Pick an overall theme and skills that students will practice while making the videos. It could be a period in music history, focusing on research and writing formal papers. Or you could do work on organizational skills while writing poetry. Make sure you write out what you want to grade the students on. We did a pre- and post-test using Survey Monkey, as well as a rubric to grade their actual writing.
- Acquire a big piece of green cloth or art paper and attach it to a blank wall (Ta-da! Green screen!)
- Before each class, make sure you have the iPads turned on and charged. Try to make sure you have a couple of free chargers hanging around your room just in case a device needs charging.
- Make sure you have pencils and paper as students are brainstorming project ideas and planning out the details for their video.
- Hang the green screen. (Try to get at least part of the floor covered as well. It will give the students more room to work with.)
- Make sure you have the computer and projector up and have the backdrops ready for them to choose.

During Class

- Go over the plan and rules for the upcoming weeks of class. If you are collaborating with your colleagues, before the project starts, discuss which rules need to carry over into every classroom, to keep continuity. You might have some other regulations for your specific class, but there are probably general rules that can carry over into all classes to keep expectations the same.
- Have students brainstorm and research the topic they chose. It could be the history of dance, the life of a famous figure in history, or the states of liquid. They could do this on their devices, or if you are working with your computer teacher, they could help you, thereby devoting time in the computer lab to do this research on student-safe search engines.
- Have them write down all the research and facts they find and begin to write either a script or a piece of music that they will perform on camera. Paper and pencil will be used to do the initial brainstorming and layout. Have a writing software open such as Microsoft Word, Google Docs, or even a notes app like Evernote or Apple's Notes app to make them available for every class to start writing down their research and organizing their scripts or songs.

- If you are working with your media teacher on this project, their part in this can be the work with the more in-depth student device use. They could be the class where students find the research for their scripts and music and type it up. Then they could learn how to use iMovie with the media teacher before they start filming their videos. Our media teacher also used it as a time to give the pre- and post-test via Survey Monkey because they had the tools to do so.
- If you are working with your PE teacher, enlist them to work on movements for the video. Students can learn how to put moves together that will work into a fluid dance or a visually engaging video. They also will be able to learn movements that they can do on a green screen that can be seen on the backdrop for the video.
- In music, when writing the lyrics to go with the piece, have students create an accompaniment track to go with their video. This activity can be the ultimate ending to a unit on songwriting or music theory that is a final product to show the rest of the world the knowledge they learned during this class time.
  o This would also be an excellent time to have the students choose images to use in their video editing. Give them a rundown of how to use the green screen so they understand how to use it in the editing process.
- Give students a checklist of everything they need to do before they can start filming. This checklist could look like the following:
  o Finish your research on the topic. Please have at least ten facts or statements written down that you could use for your music video.
  o Write a two-page song with lyrics that include the ten facts and statements about the topic. Make it creative and keep it fun! This paper will need to be in final form typed up, size 12-point Times New Roman font, double spaced, and printed on regular printer paper.
  o Create an accompaniment track that follows your lyrics. Make it one fluid piece of music.
    ▪ You can use creative tools such as GarageBand, Medly (medlylabs.com), or Quaver's QGrooves to sequence a track together using prerecorded loops of music.
    ▪ Make sure to export to an audio track for recording and voice-over purposes later!
  o Choreograph a movement piece that will last the length of your song. Use the lyrics to guide your movements and make sure you do not have any awkward pauses or silence! Make sure everything flows together and is well-practiced.
  o Sign up for green screen time and get ready!
    ▪ If you need any props, now would be an excellent time to get them together before you get in front of the green screen. You will have limited time to do it later!

- Have students spend a class or two filming! Everyone gets time at the green screen and projected background images to film their videos
  o Also, provide a quiet area for them to do any voice-over recording at editing time.
- Have them edit in media class.
- Get classes together to watch everyone's videos.

Assessment Tip: Assess students on their final videos and their songs (lyric and accompaniment track.)

Make Your Own Projector

Recommended Grades: 5–9
Difficulty: Moderate
Time: 20 min.–1 hr.
Objective: Students will problem-solve how to present their work differently.

Resources
- Mobile device
- Cardboard box
- Duct tape
- Magnifying glass
- X-acto knife
- Scissors

Projectors are still hard to find for some music educators. It's startling sometimes when you think how many of us now consider projectors to be a staple in every classroom. I was in a workshop one time where one of the teachers was concerned that they were not going to be able to do any anything with the digital resources that they were learning about because they didn't have a projector. So, I built them a projector right then and there. Technology does not need to be the shiniest piece of metal or plastic. It can be a cardboard box with a magnifying glass to project an image or a cup to turn up the volume on your phone. Imagine giving students the challenge of finding a way to show the class a video of an orchestra performance? Or a way to project their music to a larger screen? Giving students the option of constructing their visual system for performance includes engineering, critical thinking, collaboration, planning, and more from the STEAM mindset. This activity can also provide multiple devices that can project a visual onto a wall or board for more extensive operations.

Before Class
- Gather supplies you need for this project (listed in "Resources") from a craft or home improvement supply store.

FIGURE 3.5 An example of a make your own projector project (Photo Credit C. Dwinal)

- Do your research on how to create one of these projectors. You can find direction on sites like WikiHow. If you can, practice making one yourself before you do this with students so you'll know how to guide them during class time. You can also use it as a real example for students to see as they make their own.
- Put the smaller materials in bins on tables in an emptier part of the room, then put the larger items such as boxes in piles next to the containers.
- I also suggest having a few mobile devices ready with videos to show in the projectors for testing purposes. You can use YouTube, or download a video to the video player app on your device.

During Class
- Present a problem. For example, suppose that you do not have enough projectors to show all of the students' diagrams of the anatomy of specific instruments..
  - First, have students create a sample project based on what they have been learning in class. It could be videos on a musical style or diagrams of a specific instrument's anatomy.
  - Take students through how to build the projectors and set expectations on what the next class times are going to look like (e.g., how to get materials from

the bins, how to work together as a team, what goals they need to meet for this activity, etc.).
- o Examples of some of the goals for this project could be:
  - Plan out how you want your projected part of this project to look. Sketch out the diagrams on paper and pencil first.
  - Using Sketch.IO, work on your diagram. Draw out the instrument and then label it correctly with all the parts.
  - When you have completed your diagram, save it to your shared folder, and get together with your team to start building.
  - Complete your projector as a team, then using an iPod Touch, put together a presentation of all of your diagrams and put it into your projector.
  - Explore everyone's diagrams around the room!
- Have them build the projectors in teams.
- Another fun activity would be to have students build projectors individually or in small groups to be able to play videos of different orchestra groups or other types of performing ensembles like a marching band or a jazz quartet at the same time!
  - o Gather a collection of videos of different ensembles playing a style of music they enjoy.
  - o Assign each group of students a few specific videos.
  - o Have them build the projector.
  - o Once they have built it, ask students to watch the assigned videos and answer the following questions:
    - What kind of ensemble is this?
    - What instruments do you see?
    - Listen to the music. What do you hear?
    - Where is this music being played?

To Make This Projector (Find Directions on WikiHow)
- Take a cardboard box and make sure it is taped up tightly on one side. Leave the other side open for now.
- Take off the magnifying glass handle and track the glass on the front side of your box.
- Using an X-acto knife, cut out the hole you just traced the magnifying glass with.
- Glue the glass on the inside of the box over the hole.
- Using a paper clip, create a phone/iPod touch stand if your phone does not already have a kickstand or PopSocket.
- On the device, turn on whatever you would like projected. Place your device in the box with the screen facing the magnifying glass.
- Close the box tightly and turn out all the lights.
- Projector party!

Challenge: Can they build a better and bigger one? What features would they add?

Assessment Tip: Assess students on their critical thinking and problem-solving skills based on how they built their projector to present their work.

Story Movie

Recommended Grades: 5–12
Difficulty: Expert
Time: 20 min. to 2 or 3 class periods
Objective: Students will demonstrate an understanding of the connection between music and the plot of a story by creating their video.

Resources

- Computer
- Projector
- Speakers
- GarageBand or QuaverMusic.com
- iMovie, Windows Movie Maker, or Stop Motion App
- https://videos.pexels.com
- Individual devices (Preferably laptops or iPads)

I'm a sucker for a good story, especially when it is set to GREAT music. I don't think I've ever looked at Jurassic Park *the same way after seeing some of the famous scenes with and without the underscoring. How do you react when you hear the creepy music, and you know a dinosaur is coming? Music can take an excellent movie and make it a blockbuster, or it can sometimes be its downfall. It is also a perfect way to engage students. What student wouldn't enjoy having creative control over every aspect of their movie? You could also collaborate with homeroom teachers and other specialists to make an all-around fantastic film with a perfect musical score. You can also relate it to careers in music: students who are interested in movies and TV may find new future occupations. This activity could go in a whole bunch of different directions, and it's up to you to take it as far as you want.*

Before Class

- Make sure that the devices students will be using are up-to-date and have all the necessary tools downloaded to them. You might need your tech department's help on this one if they are managing the devices. Give them the list of software as suggested in "Resources" so they can install them for you.
- Suggest a few stock video sites such as https://videos.pexels.com for students to access pre-made video clips if you don't want them to make their own. You can have them go to the website to get what they want, or select and download a few to a shared drive folder that students can access when needed. Places like QuaverMusic.com have pre-made video clips along with the tools to help you score the piece. If you want to get

fancy, take some well-known animated clips and take out the vocals and any other noises so students can add their own music and vocals.

- Work with your tech specialists or coaches to make sure you have the proper tools to create videos. Some video makers might have limitations or need specific plug-ins to work correctly. This department would be able to help you navigate through them.
- Teach students about the art of film scoring before you start this activity. There are some great videos, especially on YouTube, that you could show to your students to demonstrate these possible life paths for them. Have them listen to the likes of John Williams and Hans Zimmerman to get a feel for what movie scoring can do. Play some short clips that have the music and no vocals (Disney Pixar Shorts have great examples!) to show students the power a piece of music has on a film. Discuss implications for the power of a melody on a character or plot of a movie.
- Before the class period, charge the devices! You do not want someone's device to die on them halfway through the period. Make sure to have a couple of charging stations at the ready just in case.
- Make sure the student's work can be opened on each device if they are rented out devices. If you are 1:1 have students save their work straight to their file storage preferences under a saved file name that they will remember for later.

How to Do the Project

- Preface this by showing students about film scorers. This lesson is a great career connection for them to see that there are more jobs in the music industry besides pop star, music teacher, or studio musician.
- Another great connection is the power music plays on a story or character. As suggested above, get some of Disney Pixar's short videos. Watch a few and start a discussion on how the music affects the story. Play one without the music and sounds so students can hear the difference. What about the music made them feel differently? How did they feel different listening to the video without music or sounds? Why did they feel different?
- For video content in this project, you can have three options: Have them choose between pre-made stock videos, creating stop motion pieces (this is a little more time consuming; could be done in collaboration with the art teacher), or they could create their live videos (which might be a little easier but still take some work).
- The teaching objective is to create videos accompanied by scoring that students have composed using music software, that properly sets the scene or the character's motive.
- One possible idea is to create and score a 1-minute video clip of a character walking down a busy hallway before school starts. The music and sounds must be reflective of what the character is doing on the screen and must illustrate some emotion.
- Have students plan their video and create an outline for how everything will appear and what the overall theme is. Then, plan a shooting schedule if needed.

- If they are filming their video, planning out the story will take a little more effort. Students must plan out the following:
  - Overall theme
  - What the characters look like
  - What each character is doing in every part of the video
  - What sets, costumes, and props will they need
  - If they are making stop motion, what art supplies they will need for their video
  - What the shooting schedule will be like and how much they can shoot per class
  - How much time it will take them to score their video. Can they have group members working on the music at the same time as the rest are filming?
- If they have the option to choose a pre-made video clip:
  - Where is the source of their video? Do they have the write citations to be able to give proper credit in their films?
  - Have they chosen a piece that is 1 minute? If they need to do any video editing, how much? How long do they think it will take?
  - Does the video help to complete the objective?

- Have students shoot their video and let them know that they do not need any audio at first. They should be able to take out any ambient sounds in the video editor they are using before adding in their own audio. Make sure to teach them how to cut out any lingering audio on iMovie/Windows Movie Maker before they start scoring.
- After they have finished the visuals for their video, have them watch their silent videos on the projector. Then reflect on how the audio should sound. It would be best to have them write down where the sounds and music should go while they do this. Have them either type it up on their device using a note-taking app or write it down on paper.
- Students will now compose a piece of music to go along with their videos, using Pro Tools, GarageBand, or even QuaverMusic.com. Some recommended requirements for the composition part of this activity:
  - You must use at least three layers of audio in your piece. One must be the music, one must be your voice-over, and one must be any ambient sounds needed, such as the sound of walking or background chatter. It is encouraged to add in an extra layer of music for more depth in your video.
  - Make sure each piece aligns with what is playing on the screen. It will not have as full an effect if the timing is off. Work on the smaller cuts and minor details to make this work.
  - Stick with a similar style of music for continuity in the video.
  - Create drama with at least two tempo changes and two dynamic changes in your piece.
  - Be creative! You do not need to do what everyone else is doing. Think outside the box.
- After they have finished creating their sounds, compress the audio file and export as an MP3 and then import into their iMovie/Windows Movie Maker.

- Adjust and cut audio to align it with what is going on in the video. Encourage students to take their time!
- When the students are done with their videos, and have completed all goals, have them export as a MOV file. Then they can either email them to you or drop them into a shared cloud folder.
- Take everyone's short films and create a reel. Have a movie day!
- If you want to take this a step further, have students reflect on their classmate's videos. How was the video? How did the music sound? Did the music and movie fit together? You can create a reflection worksheet with some of the following example questions to spark reflection:
  o What was one strength in your classmate's videos?
  o What is one idea that you found in your classmate's videos that you hope to be able to do yourself if you do this again?
  o How was the process of creating your project? Was there anything confusing? Was there anything fun?
  o After watching your video on the big screen, What is one constructive criticism you have for your project?
  o Reflect on those who do this for a living. How do you think this would be for a career?

Assessment Tip: Assess students on their overall video project taking special care to look at the audio and music they created and scored for the project.

Found Sounds

Recommended Grades: 6–12
Difficulty: Moderate
Time: 60–120 min.
Objective: Students will show learned knowledge of how objects can make sounds through the creation of their own found sounds piece.

Resources
- Computer
- Projector
- iMovie or Quaver's QSoundFx
- Speakers
- Mobile devices
- Slinky
- Recyclable materials

An important point to make to students in music class is the fact that there is more out there for careers in music beyond pop star or world-class classical musician. If they want to do something different in music, they can be anything from an audio engineer to a Foley artist to a music supervisor. Ten years from now, there will be even more jobs that have yet to be invented. Sixty percent of the students that we teach in classes every year will have jobs that our society has not created yet. Maybe in the future, there will be a digital soundwaves DJ? Or a found sounds specialist? Found sounds have a significant connection to STEAM, which has become an integral part of the educational foundation. Administrations are pressuring music teachers to integrate more STEAM initiatives into the short amount of time they have with students every week. Found sounds have become a great go-to project for a lot of music teachers, especially at the younger grade levels for the science of sound connections. It makes it easier to integrate the push for the science connections into such a deep-rooted traditional pedagogy that music is. In this project, students will take a more in-depth look into the career of Foley artist, get a more detailed look into the science of sound connections in the field, and create a final product that shows off their learning.

Before Class

- You will need to rent out mobile devices for your students through your media teacher or technology department. If you are a 1:1 school, you will need to alert the students and their teacher to make sure they bring their devices for the next few classes.
- Bookmark a couple of useful videos on YouTube about the art of Foley work (these can be links you can put into directions for the students for them to watch individually or you can watch them together as a group before the project). Two great recommendations are
  - "The Magic of Making Sound" by Great Big Story
  - "Foley Artist Gary Hecker" by Giray Bayer
- Make sure that the devices students will be using are up to date and have all the necessary tools downloaded to them. You might need the help of your tech department for this. If you are on a Chromebook, a program like WeVideo might be the best bet for your students in this project. PC laptops and desktops would use Windows Movie Maker, Apple Laptops and iPads would use iMovie. As said before, it is whatever your tech department feels would be best. They are the ones that will be supporting you if any tech fails, so you want to make sure that you work with them for what is most compatible with the district network.
- Collect a variety of recycled materials that are safe for students to use. When I did something similar, I used the recycling bin that was filled by our art teacher with all kinds of recyclables. You could ask colleagues to borrow some of the materials in their containers or put out a call to parents/guardians to help bring in some of the materials. Some suggestions for materials would be:
  - Construction paper or printer paper
  - Clean paper plates and cups
  - Aluminum foil
  - Pie plates

- Boxes
- Pencils and broken pens
- String
- Tape
- And the list goes on—use your imagination

- Let students know that they will be working on a project that will require them to make different sounds than what they usually hear and if students would like to bring in extra materials, make sure they clear it with their parents first. Let them know they can drop items off in your room when they first come to school. Make them aware that a lot of what comes in will be used for Foley work so it would be best if it did not need to go back. If materials do need to go back, then have the students put their names on them and keep them in a safe place until they are picked up after the project.

- Create a playlist of silent videos on YouTube; if you go the video editor route, it will be a fun history connection to use silent videos since that can lead to talking about the film industry—when it first started and how it has evolved along with the music that goes into it. If you want to take it a bit of a different direction, you can have students recreate one of the silent movie clips and then dub it over with their sounds. Programs like Quaver in the suggestion list are self-contained and have everything the students need for this in one place. Video editors will need for students to either create their own movie or borrow a clip from a free site.

- Create a worksheet using Google Docs or Word to be done on their mobile devices or with paper and pencil. This worksheet will have the names of the members of their group, the clip they are using, then a list of the sounds that they need to fill with the materials they will be using next to it. The worksheet could look something like this:
  - Group members
  - Name of the clip used for video
  - Sounds
    - Horse neighing
    - Someone running
    - A baby crying
    - A high five
    - Whispering
    - Two people laughing
    - A pencil writing
    - Someone typing

- The period before your class comes in, cue up the videos that you would like to show to preface this project.

- Spread out any sound-making materials that you brought in for the classes to use. If students brought in any unique materials set them aside for when their group comes.

- Plan out in the room or hallway where you would like groups to work.

During Class

- When the class settles, ask the question, "How can you make the sound of someone jumping into a lake without having someone jump into a lake?"
- Ask students to discuss the question with each other first before sharing with the whole class how they would do it. (Answers could range from throwing a rock in a bucket of water to a mouth sound.)
- Introduce the idea of a Foley artist and play the videos that you have chosen.
- Discuss how you would create different sounds for movies. What could lead to a life as a Foley artist? You could also discuss how the Foley artists and movie scorers were very important, especially at the start of the film industry because at that time all films were silent.
- Show students the selection of clips or movies they can use for this project. Have them create groups and discuss which clip they would like to use. (If they are using Quaver QSoundFx the clips are already built in, if they are using iMovie/Movie Maker they can use the silent clips you found, or you can choose for them to recreate a silent movie to use after.)
- Pass out the worksheet to each group and have them write down the initial information. Once they have chosen the clip they will use, they will need to plan out the sounds that need dubbing over. It would be a great time to bring out the recyclables you have collected for students to get hands-on with and discover what will work for them.
- Another great way to use your projector during this time is to put the goals or directions for the project on the board so students can continuously be looking at them as they are working.
- Before you allow students to handle devices, remind them the following,
  Treat your devices with the same respect as you would in any other class. Make sure to keep them squarely on the floor or a table when you are using them!
- Give each group time to create a plan before having them start work on their creations. Give them time to record each sound, which they can do on their mobile devices right into Quaver or iMovie. They can record and then edit and adjust any audio they record directly in the app.
- If they are recording video themselves and not using a pre-made clip, they will need to shoot the video before working on the audio. This could be another great time for collaboration between you and a colleague. They could have students film in their classes while you work on audio!
- Once they have recorded all of their audio, have them do any final editing they need. Then they can work on adding a score to the scene. With these apps, they will need to write a short melody and play it on real instruments before recording it straight into the tools. They can use either staff paper and pencils or a notation creator such as Finale or Noteflight. Then students can use classroom instruments or band instruments to play and record their musical themes into the final video.

- Have groups export and submit their assignments to you. Then compile them into a full reel. Have each group come up and explain a little bit about their work before playing it for the class using the projector.
- Have other groups give constructive feedback on each assignment to keep the discussion going!

Assessment Tip: Using the pieces of music that the students create, assess them on their final products, taking a particular observation on the music they have created and how it fits into the finished product.

Guitar Sheet Music

Recommended Grades: 6–12
Difficulty: Moderate
Time: 2 to 3 class periods
Objective: Students will compose and perform a piece on the guitar.

Resources
- Computer
- Projector
- Musescore.org
- Speakers
- Laptops or desktop computers
- Sign up sheet for performance times.

When students want to learn guitar from me, they usually want to learn how to write music to sing and play along with, or they have a favorite song that they want to play over and over just like their favorite rock star. The usual progression is they want to learn how to play their favorite songs and then learn how to create their music. I have several students who learned basic guitar from me after school. After learning single notes and scales, they then learn basic chords, which allows them to start playing and singing songs. Several of them have gone on and bought guitars of their own. I get videos from their parents, showing me the songs they create. It is a new outlet for them to enjoy, initially prompted by seeing their favorite on-screen character playing guitar or a wish to be like their favorite band, but once they learn an instrument they can play for the rest of their lives. They can continue to love the art of making music no matter if they are playing for a crowd, playing for themselves, or playing for the family on holiday.

Before Class
- This activity would be best to end a guitar unit in a general music class, or as an activity during a guitar class. All students should have access to a guitar for this. You most

likely will have a guitar for everyone if this is a guitar class. If not, you can always look to your local music shop for some loaners, or ask students to bring their own.

- Students should have the prerequisite knowledge of being able to play basic guitar, like single notes, a few scales, and a couple basic chords.
- If they do not have individual devices, you will need to rent out the computer lab or a cart of mobile devices for at least two classes.
- Double-check your Internet connection to make sure everything is running quickly.
  - If you suspect your Internet might be having an issue, head to https://fast.com, and do an Internet speed test. The more Mbps you have, the better.
- Write down what the expectations and goals are for this assignment:
  - Objective: To create a short piece of music using the Musescore program, which you will perform for the teacher.
    - Your piece of music be at least 16 measures long.
    - Your music must have a guitar and vocal part; only having one will lose points.
    - Your piece must have at least two chords.
    - Your melody line must fit your singing comfort level.
    - Choose a tempo that fits your comfort level.
    - Take the time to practice.
    - Make sure to sign up for a performance slot.
- If you are uncomfortable working with any of the technology, alert your tech coordinator that you are about to do this project and ask for them to come to help you if you need it.
- On the day of class, make sure all of the devices have access to Musescore.org. It is a cloud-based software so there should be no downloading or uploading. It is just a matter of making sure the machines have enough working memory to load the program, and that the Wi-Fi access point in your area of the building can take a full class of students getting on at the same time.
- Create a sign-up sheet for students to come to play for you individually.
- If needed, print out the goal and tasks for this activity. If you would like to save paper, put it into a Google Doc, and share the link with the class. You can also project the goals and objectives for the project on the board, so students have a constant visual reminder of what they need to accomplish for this activity.
- If you have a class set of guitars, bring them out for students ahead of time. If not, send a reminder to bring them for these classes to complete the project.

During Class

- Have students warm up together with scales and a few strumming exercises. You can use the books and warm-ups the students are already using in the unit.
- Explain that the goal of the activity is to create a short piece of music using the Musescore program, which they will perform for the teacher. Then go on to explain

what tasks they need to complete to meet the goal. (You could provide students with a goal worksheet as well.)

- Review with students how to write a melody with basic chord progressions (such as I–V–I). If they need a more extensive review, then spend a class period or so beforehand going through the process and have students practice before this activity.
- Get on Musescore.org and show students how to operate the program. Together create a short warm-up and play it together as a class. Then have them recreate the warm-up themselves for individual practice.
- Make sure each student has access to a device and a guitar. Allow them to disperse into the room and ask them to watch the noise level. (You could use the noise level meter as suggested earlier if you want to give students a visual for them to know how loud they get.)
- Give students time to apply the knowledge they have been learning in class. Circulate the room to guide and answer any questions they may have as they are working on the project.
- When a student feels they are close to being done and are confident with performing for you, ask them to sign up for a playing time slot. Then have them practice until it is their turn to play.
- After students have played for you and have printed out their music to turn in to you, provide a new piece of music for them to practice until their classmates finish. Then have the whole class come together to play their new music.

Assessment Tip: Assess students on their performance and the printed sheet music they turn in.

4

Interactive Boards and TVs

FIGURE 4.1 Interactive boards come in all different types of setups from interactive touch boards to ones with an interactive projector as pictured above (Photo Credit C. Dwinal)

Visual Scores

Recommended Grades: PreK–7
   Difficulty: Moderate
   Time: 5–20 min.

Interactive Visual Ideas for Musical Classroom Activities. Catherine Dwinal, Oxford University Press (2020). © Oxford University Press.
DOI: 10.1093/oso/9780190929855.001.0001

Objective: The class will demonstrate aural musicianship by creating visual score representations of a piece of music they are listening to.

Resources

- Computer
- Interactive board
- Speakers
- YouiDraw, Smart Notebook, ActivInspire software
- Pencils and paper.

A visual score is a simple line drawing that allows younger students to follow along and better understand a more significant piece of music while seeing the more profound meaning within. Think of it as a listening map. When I use these with my students, I want them to go beyond just listening, so breaking it down into a more straightforward, visual way is helpful for them. An activity like this makes listening to music more engaging to the students as they map out the songs with the instruments they hear, the dynamics, the tempo, and even the form. I do a few different versions of this activity throughout the year with my students. My favorite uses "Danse Macabre." Students love hearing the spooky song that gets them into a Halloween mood, and it helps them practice listening for form patterns in longer songs. We divide the screen into fourths and label them based on the different sections of the song and then draw a picture on the part of the paper that corresponds with the section we hear. Then we go on to celebrate the rest of the spooky holiday! Listening activities are the best activity to do together as a class, then individually. You can have students lead the full class activity before they break off for their individual practice. In this lesson, students listen to music and use their critical thinking skills uniquely and musically!

Before Class

- Pick your music. You can go for pretty much any musical style with this activity, from rock to reggae. It tends to work best with classical pieces. This activity can allow you to break down pieces from different composers, genres, and musical periods. Make sure to have the songs either downloaded as MP3s or have them saved to a playlist on YouTube. I suggest music like:
  - "Danse Macabre"
  - Beethoven's Fifth Symphony
  - "Blue Danube"
  - *Carnival of the Animals*
  - *The Nutcracker*

- Double-check to make sure your board works with the drawing tool you have chosen. If you have a SMART board, you can use the Notebook software to draw on your board. Promethean boards also have a drawing tool built into their ActivInspire software that can do the same thing.
- Check your interactivity on the board. You might need to recalibrate if the mouse is not clicking on the right area. These writing programs require the board to be very accurate when using them to make things a little more legible for the work you are doing.
- Before each class, make sure the piece of music you want students to listen to is cued up (YouTube and iTunes usually have great audio-only videos like the ones suggested). If you are using a cloud-based music player, you most likely will need to play the file all the way through to load it fully up just in case your Internet is a bit slow.
- Make sure your board has the drawing tool up, and it is operational (you might need to calibrate it before class again).

During Class

- For this first activity, you are going to build a full visual score.
  - Play through a section of the piece and start by making marks on the board for the steady beat as students listen.
  - After the section finishes, ask them "How could we take what we listened to and make it into something that we can see? Can we draw it?" See if any of the students can figure out what the marks are that you just drew on the board in the previous step.
  - Play through the same section of the piece again. Ask students to listen for the rhythm. Take volunteers to draw the rhythmic line out on the board for you on the bottom. Have students perform the rhythm using body percussion and see if it matches up with what is written in the song.
  - Next, have them list all the instruments that they hear in the piece. Create a line for each of the instruments listed.
  - Play through the same section of the piece again. Ask students to listen for the melodic lines of each of the instruments that were listed. Take volunteers to draw the melodies for each instrument on the board in their respective rows.
  - Play the section one more time and have students follow along to the song using the visual that they just drew. Ask the question, "Do you think we accurately represented the song here on the board?
  - Pass out paper and pencil (or if you have access to mobile devices, sites like Sketch.io are great for students to use as a different way to follow along).
  - Play the piece again, and have students draw their visual scores. Have students volunteer to come up and explain their thought process after the music is complete.

- Another activity suggestion would be to do more of a symbol-based visual score. This one goes with the "Danse Macabre."
  - Play through a section of the piece and start by dividing the board into fourths. Then label each section with what each part represents; in this case, it would be a skeleton, a violin, footsteps, and a ghost.
  - After the song finishes, ask them the question, "Can we keep track of how many times we hear each section?"
  - As a class, come up with a movement that they can do every time that they hear one of the specific sections. Take two student volunteers to be the ones to make the check marks when they see students make different movements.
  - Play through the same song again. Ask students to listen and make a move when they hear the beginning of the section that corresponds with the movement.
  - Pass out paper and pencil (or if you have access to mobile devices, sites like Sketch. io are great to have students use as a different way to follow along). Have students divide their paper into fourths and title each section.
  - Play the piece again, and have students count each of the movements that they hear themselves. After they have completed their maps, play through the music one more time and count it all together (including the one that they did together on the board). Who got it right? Were there any incorrect sections?
  - You can vary this activity with a different musical selection. Just make sure to divide up the board with how many sections the piece needs.

Assessment Tip: Have students self-assess their visual scores based on how well they followed the melodic contour, the instruments they heard, and any other criteria you want them to cover. Go over the piece together as a class and have them evaluate their work individually. Assess them on their self-evaluations.

Make Your Own SMART Board Activities

Recommended Grades: PreK–8
  Difficulty: Moderate
  Time: 5–35 min.
  Objective: Students will demonstrate learned concept knowledge through completion of interactive activities presented on the board.

Resources
- Computer
- SMART board with Notebook software
- Speakers

The SMART board has become a way of creating digital tools for many teachers. It is an innovative way to customize activities for the music classroom. You can change up

FIGURE 4.2 Smartboards are one of the more popular types of interactive boards in the classroom (Photo Credit C. Dwinal)

manipulatives, add in different composing grids, and make full interactive games. The first time I created activities in the SMART Notebook software, my lesson went up a notch from drawing lines to represent beats on the whiteboard to an interactive scene using ants as the beats and blades of grass as the rests. When I was substitute teaching, I was asked to help the kindergarten teachers during testing time. I took classes to the media center during testing and did activities on the SMART board in there for 45 to 50 minutes while the teachers pulled individual students out for testing. I would have free rein to do whatever I wanted with the students during these couple of weeks. I relied heavily on creating a lot of the material that I would use. Some of it was not necessarily music-related, but I could make anything from a math counting game to a "find the states on the map" puzzle. Having something that students could interact with promotes better engagement!

Before Class

- Download the SMART Notebook software to your device. Here is the Getting Started Instructions from the SMART company on how to use the software:
  https://support.smarttech.com/en/software/smart-notebook
- Develop some activities to use on your board. The best place to start is manipulatives. You can create a multiplying character that students can continue to drag and drop into a grid or pattern.

- Make sure your computer has all the correct interactivity drivers installed for the board. This trick might be something you need to have your technology department take care of for you.
- Turn on your board and make sure that all the interactivity works. Test out your activities on the board to make sure that they operate the way you intended them to work.
- Before each class, make certain your activity works with your SMART board. If it is not interacting, make sure all wires are plugged in tightly!

During Class

- Create a screen that has a multiplying character on it. Also, make sure there is some grid or a specific place to drag the characters. Have students work together to create rhythms, and if you have a staff, you can create melodies as well. Have students use instruments or body percussion to play what they have created.
- Draw a Venn diagram and key topics or words that belong in each. Have students categorize where the keywords or topics belong.
- Brainstorm! You can have all kinds of brainstorming grids ready for in-depth discussions during your lessons. Some suggestions for grid starters are:
  o Create a grid with pictures that represent each instrument family. Have a bank of keywords to put in each box for each family. Have students put each keyword into each box where it belongs and use the draw tool to add to more to each keyword.
  o Create a KWL chart (What We Know, What We Want to learn, What We Learned). Have students write down their answers in the different columns and take a screenshot to save for later.
  o Create a set of columns for different concepts like musical periods, composers, and song titles for students to fill in.
  o Have students answer a series of questions in different parts of the screen.

Assessment Tip: Assess students on their participation in the class activity using the board.

Interactive Morning Message

Recommended Grades: PreK–12
Difficulty: Beginner
Time: 5–15 min.
Objective: Students will show prior learned knowledge by answering questions presented in the welcome message.

Resources

- Computer
- Interactive board
- Google Docs or Microsoft Word

When I first started working on my classroom management skills, I began to put welcome messages on the board as part of my daily routine: short messages for students to read as they were coming in and sitting down that would tell them a little about the week ahead. A message was only a short paragraph but would welcome students, tell them a bit of what to expect, and perhaps give them an activity to do as soon as they came into class to maximize time. It is something that all general classroom teachers do so I was bringing a little something familiar to them when they came into my room. I now also use Google Docs and can quickly put up the message for whichever class is about to walk through the door. The time it takes me to keep up with these messages is about 20 minutes a week. I have six Google Docs all labeled with the grade level and then a message for them that covers the week. I keep it open for the grade level and then close it at the end of the day. I feel more organized, and my students know the class expectations from the moment they walk through the door. The message on the board gives students directions, something to think about, and they feel welcomed as soon as they come in. I make it interactive by having students write answers to questions or drag manipulatives into boxes to answer polls that I pose. You could always go a step further and do a QR code that students could scan to get a specific activity to do as soon as class starts. There are a lot of opportunities to get the learning going as soon as you walk through the door even while you take attendance and work through the standard beginning-of-class needs. Students can start discussions and work on "Do-Nows" as class begins so you can use the short amount of time you have with them as efficiently as possible!

Before Class

- You will need to create a folder for all your messages. If you are using Google Docs, then go into your Google Drive and click New, then Folder. You could title it "Welcome Messages" or "Morning Messages." If you are using Microsoft Word, right-click on your desktop and click New Folder and label it something similar. Google Docs or Microsoft Word are the most efficient tools to create welcome messages for each grade level or class you have for the week. Make it welcoming and give them a little hint of what they will be experiencing in music for that lesson. Some quick examples could be:
  - "Welcome Music Adventurers! Get ready for another class of playing, singing, dancing, and learning! This week we are going to use our knowledge of notes and rests and learn where they go on the staff. Get ready because our favorite instruments will come out today!"
  - "Good morning one and all! Make sure to have your projects turned in before we start the lesson for the day. Today is all about the groovy 1960s! Let's get ready for some peace, love, and rock 'n' roll. Get your writing utensils ready! What is your favorite decade?"
- To make them more interactive, pose a question, and leave room for students to write answers using the board's drawing tools. Some example questions could be:
  - What is your favorite instrument? How does that instrument make a sound? Discuss with a friend.

o What musical period was Beethoven alive? Write your answer on the board!

o How many pieces of music can you name that are in the style of rock 'n' roll? Make a list with a friend.

o Take out a dry erase board and dry erase marker. Using only quarter and barred eighth notes, compose one measure of rhythm in 4/4 time. Be prepared to clap it for the class when we get the lesson rolling.

o Listen to the piece of music playing. In what period do you think this was written? What kinds of instruments can you hear? Be prepared to discuss your thoughts about the piece.

o We are continuing work on our projects today! Please take out the materials you need and get right to work. Make sure to write on the board what goal you are working on today. I'll know you have read these directions if you are working and not sitting in the circle!

o Please vote for one of the pieces on the board for the upcoming concert. Then, take out your instruments and practice warm-ups 1 and 2 on page 12 in your method books. We will be practicing the winner of the vote plus "Sleigh Ride" and "Winter Wonderland" today.

o Did you listen to music before school this morning? What kind of music was it? What are your feelings about it? Talk with a friend and find someone who listened to similar songs this morning.

- Before each class, get your message up! I always had mine stored in a Google Drive folder for easy access during class times. You might have yours saved to a folder on the desktop or a file in your SMART board programs.

- If you plan to have students writing or dragging things on the board, make sure that the interactive portion of the board is working. You might need to recalibrate the drawing pens if they are slightly off or students might have a hard time writing answers.

During Class

- The best time to have your message up is as students are entering the room. Get them in the routine of reading it themselves and following directions.

- If they are younger students, then you will most likely need to keep the words at a minimum and have a few pictures to get your message across; most likely they will need to read it together as a class. The best part about having these messages up for the younger ones is that they will start to recognize words and learn to read the full messages as the year goes on.

One of these messages might read:

"Welcome Musical Adventurers!
This week we will experience the life of Mozart. Be sure to bring your Chromebooks next week for a research activity! Today we will read a story about the composer, listen to some of his work, and play a short song we learned last week!

Ms. Dwinal"

- Older students will be able to read and follow more directions in the message. You might have some activities for them to do at that moment as the class is settling down and you are taking attendance. This activity will get them in a routine and teach them the expectations of each class time.

One of these messages might right read,

"Good Morning All
Today, please take out your instruments and warm up using page 3 in your method books. We will be practicing "Sleigh Ride" and "Carol of the Bells" for rehearsal today. Please have those ready to go. Also, remember that practice sheets are due on Friday! Please be prepared to rehearse when I hit the podium.

Ms. D."

- Or you can write a message that gives students directions regarding a project you want them to jump right into as soon as they walk in for class. Set small goals that you want them to accomplish during that period. Music educators only have a certain amount of time with their students, and every moment counts. An example of that could be,

"Hello All,
A reminder that we are working on composition projects today, which are due next week!
 Today, please work on:
 Finishing your melody lines. The computer cart is available at the front of the room for you. Please take your assigned device.
 Start working on your lyrics. Remember to save your file as a Google Doc for easy access when you are putting the whole piece together.
 Make sure to look at your goals sheet and double-check that you have completed your halfway check-in."

- Ask them to collaboratively build a melody on the board to play as a class.
- If you want students to do a more individual activity, ask them to get dry erase boards and markers (or a piece of paper and a pencil) and compose a short rhythm or melody within specific parameters that they will play in a round-robin activity at the start of class.
- If you are 1:1 with mobile devices, you can have them interact with the message in a couple of different ways:
  ○ You can have them access a Google Form that you have created to answer questions about the content of today's lesson.

- o Use Kahoot.it! Make it a game that you and the students can do together when the class starts. Have them spend the first bit of the period getting set up for it then they will be ready to play as soon as class starts.
- o Create a Poll Everywhere (polleverywhere.com) for students to answer as you are getting ready for class.
- o Create a Padlet from Padlet.com and have students post and answer questions in one collaborative space. Students can post from the message prompt and then other students can answer in the same thread.
- Post a question for students to discuss with their group members. This would be an excellent time for students listen to a piece and then reflect on it, in group discussion or individual journaling. Let's say you play a recording of a selection from Tchaikovsky's *Nutcracker Suite*. Here are some possible questions:
  - o Can you hear the themes in this piece?
  - o Who composed the *Nutcracker Suite*? What is the story?
  - o What is your favorite instrument in this piece, and why?
  - o Write your answers on the board and be prepared to discuss them with the class.
- Another listening example could be "Let it Be" by the Beatles. Some possible questions for this example:
  - Listen to the lyrics. What is this song about? What is your interpretation of the words?
  - What style of music is this? How is it different from the styles of popular music today?
  - How does the music make you feel?

Assessment Tip: Assess students on their answers to the questions in the interactive message.

Instrument Safari

Recommended Grades: K–2
Difficulty: Expert
Time: 30–45 min.
Objective: Students will exhibit knowledge of instruments of the orchestra by completing the safari activity and contributing to the discussion.

Resources
- Computer
- Interactive board
- http://listeningadventures.carnegiehall.org

Extended Activity Resources

- Plastic Easter eggs
- Cut-out photos of instruments
- Marker
- Googly eyes
- An outdoor place with excellent hiding spots

FIGURE 4.3 My little monster eggs ready to be hidden for the activity! (Photo Credit C. Dwinal)

It was spring, and the kids were begging to have class outside. I decided to go "above and beyond" the last few classes of the year as we were going over instruments of the orchestra, one of my favorite units to teach. We started with a regular class activity where students interacted with the jungle safari on the board, then I gave them a surprise activity: an outdoor hunt for the instruments they had been learning. It took the fantasy into reality and promoted a whole new level of engagement. Students were already engrossed in a story of going into the jungle to find missing instruments, and when I opened the door, they were excited to venture outside to find the instruments themselves. An absolute bonus was that students adored this website so much that I had many students ask for the URL so they could go home and play it later! I used it again a few grades later when we went more in-depth about the instrument families.

Before Class

- Check your tech! Make sure your interactive board is working. If not, contact your tech department to remedy any issues before continuing with your safari.
- Head to: http://listeningadventures.carnegiehall.org and register for a free account. This trick will allow you to save your progress as you go along just in case it takes more than one class period to go through your safari. You can play a local game each time as well, but it will not save your progress. I usually do a local game when I have students do this together as a full group because I can choose individual instrument families and focus on one part of the safari at a time.
- Prepare your students with information on the instruments of the orchestra. Draw four columns on the board and label each one with the name of each instrument family. Then discuss and write down the attributes and characteristics of each family of instruments. Review and discuss how they relate to one another. Make sure to have plenty of pictures of each instrument.

If You Are Going to Do the Extended Activity

- Using the plastic eggs and the googly eyes, create a little egg monster army. Feel free to add more decorations to the eggs if you would like. I glue on pipe cleaners, extra teeth, even pictures of other little monsters or people.
- After you have played Dr. Frankenstein, label your little monsters with instruments of the orchestra. I put the first letter of the family name on the bottom of the egg with a Sharpie so I do not get them mixed up when hiding them in different corners of the playground.
- Find pictures of each instrument on the web. Copy and paste them into a Word document and label each one with its name. After you have done that, save, print, and cut them out and place inside of their eggs for your students to discover.
- Get crafty and create signs for each instrument family area like the Brasslands and Woodwind Pond.
- If you are doing the extended activity, on the day of class, go outside and hide your eggs in a rarely used part of the playground or field. I have a separate area of the school fields near my room where I can hide the eggs. If it's a rainy day and you don't want it to ruin your fun, get permission from your administration and collaborate with a couple of teachers to hold your instrument egg hunt within the school!
- Make sure to load the website and project it onscreen before students walk in and make sure everything is in working order!
- When students are coming in, greet them at the door with sounds of the jungle playing in the background, and have them put on their invisible "safari hats" to get into character. If you have the budget and want to go a little further, places like bulk order stores have plastic safari hats you can get in bulk and inexpensively!

- Place the students either in rows or in a horseshoe shape around the screen, so everyone has an equal chance of seeing everything and being included if they review the characteristics of each of the instrument families. This activity will help them on their safari a little later!
- Take them on safari! Students can become very immersed in the story. It gives plenty of opportunity for you as the teacher to get them to think more critically about the puzzles and challenges presented through the adventure. Be their guide through the experience; really get into character!
- If you are short on time and cannot do all of the adventures, the game allows you to choose where you want to focus for the day so you can break it up into different parts. It is not as immersive as doing the whole thing, but still useful.
- The interactive board will come in very handy during this safari because there are choices and challenges along the way. Choose students to come up and be the ones to make the decisions. There are plenty of opportunities for many students in the class to get a turn. You also can create opportunities for teams to get together to have more in-depth discussions and finish challenges.
- When you have reached the final performance in the game, this is an excellent lead-in into the extended activity. Some examples of how to introduce it could be:
  o "I was going to bring the instruments here to see you, but they accidentally got out! We need to go outside and find them!"
  o "I had instruments here for you to see, but they were stolen by some sneaky little eggs who wanted them for a snack! We need to find those eggs and get those instruments back! Come on!"
  o "Violet and I brought the safari to you; let's go outside. The instruments are hiding on the playground!"
- Take the students outside and have them get into teams to search for instrument eggs to bring to the stage. Consider it something like an Easter egg hunt. You can assign each group to a different area to find the eggs.
- When each team identifies an instrument from their area and brings them back to the "stage," you can do a few things:
  o When they bring one back, have them read the instrument label on the egg and show you the picture. They can identify the instrument family which it belongs in, mime how to play the instrument, and also describe the sound that each produces.
  o When all the eggs are located, have students sit in a traditional orchestra seating style until everyone comes back with an instrument. Play the piece of music again and have them mime their instruments.
- To clean up, have them put their instrument pictures back in the eggs and into a basket as they leave.
- A follow-up activity to this would be for students to complete a worksheet where they categorize all the instruments into their respective family categories. You could also create an interactive activity through one of the board programs such as SMART Notebook. Divide the screen into four sections and name each one with the instrument

family name. Put down all the instrument manipulatives you can think of and have them drag and drop the instruments into the right categories.

Assessment Tip: After students have completed the safari, give them a worksheet to test their learned knowledge about the instrument families and which instruments belong in which family (see Figure 4.4).

Instrument Safari Worksheet

Name:
Date:
Class:

In each column, describe what makes each instrument family unique. After you have completed that, list as many instruments that belong in that family as you can.

Brass	Woodwind	Percussion	String
Description:	Description:	Description:	Description:
Instruments:	Instruments:	Instruments:	Instruments:

FIGURE 4.4 Worksheet example to use for activity.

Musical Community Activity

Recommended Grades: K–3
Difficulty: Moderate
Time: 15 min.–1 hr.
Objective: The class will create a piece of music that is reflective of their local community through digital and nondigital means.

Resource

- Computer
- Interactive board
- Speakers
- Isle of Tune
- Individual devices with writing app or paper and pencil

This activity is great to do, especially in the kindergarten or first-grade level when children are beginning to learn more about their community and what is around them. You can turn this into a collaboration between you and the general classroom teachers. Show the students that the world around them is musical, and let your music class provide a venue for them to practically apply the knowledge they are learning about their local communities. The first- and second-grade teachers in my schools have a great unit about the community where they take field trips throughout the year to explore places like the library, police station, and fire station.

Before Class

- Make sure that IsleofTune.com works with your system. You might still need to use Adobe Flash for this. If not, you can use a mobile device like an iPad and mirror your display on to your board through apps such as Splashtop or Doceri.
- Check your interactivity on the board. You might need to recalibrate if the mouse is not clicking on the right area. This program requires the board to be very accurate when using it to put the moving parts of the town in the spots you would like them to be.
- You want to create a new island. Then make sure you can place all of the different sounds on the board.
- Make sure that you rent out the individual devices beforehand if you need to.
- If you would like to go a step further, get a map together of where famous town landmarks such as the police or fire stations are in your local area. Get that going before you do this activity with students.
- Before each class, make sure IsleofTune.com is up and ready to go. You need to click a few buttons to get into the site.
- Make sure all individual devices are on, charged, and ready to go.

- If you are using paper and pencil instead of individual devices, make sure you have everything laid out for class ahead of time.

During Class

- Ask students to brainstorm some places they can find in their local community (e.g., library, fire station, high school, etc.). Write them on the board. Ask questions: Why are these places important to a community? What roles do they play?
  - o Let students know the goal of this activity is to write a piece of music about places in their community.
  - o Bring up the Isle of Tune on the projector and show them how to make a piece of music by first placing the road in a pattern on the board. Then they can place the houses and trees along the path to create the sounds. Then they have to put cars on the road to create the music.
  - o Ask students to describe the community that they see playing music in front of them. Write a short story about it.
- Bring out the individual devices and ask students to build their musical community through the app. Once they have created their piece of music, have them write out a short story about the community they have created (ask students to include many places they would have in a local community). Ask for volunteers to share what they have created.
  - o If you want to go a step in a different direction, overlay a map of the essential places are that are in their own community and have students create a virtual community around it.
  - o Share the completed pieces of music and stories with the school community around them.

Assessment Tip: In this activity, students are creating a story with music. Assess their final piece, paying attention to how well the melodic contour flows and follows the story they created.

Interactive Games

Recommended Grades: K–7
Difficulty: Beginner
Time: 5–20 min.
Objective: Students will demonstrate knowledge of basic music theory and musicianship skills through interacting with visuals on the board.

Resources

- Computer
- Interactive board

- Speakers
- QuaverMusic.com, Blob Chorus app, StoryBots.com, Teoria.com (find more resources in the index)

Games can be an interactive and straightforward way to incorporate your board into instruction while learning about and appreciating music. There are hundreds of options on the Internet, and most of them can be used in a multitude of different approaches that are beyond their original intended use. I have a whole slew of activities and resources that specifically go along with the lessons I plan for the day. From quick 5-minute games and activities that I do on the board, to more in-depth discussions and activities using the board as a visual, there are many opportunities for assessment. One of my favorites is always using QuaverMusic.com's Staff Champion, a note naming game that comes in different forms and difficulty levels. It has two modes, either Teacher Mode that is untimed and unscored, or Game Mode, which puts 30 seconds on the clock and gives students a small selection of answers to choose from. We do this activity in a few different settings, from a quick 5-minute activity together at the end of class to small group activity. At some points, I even include it into a center where students can compete against each other.

Before Class
- Some of the better games and activities most likely come with a price, like Quaver and Story Bots. Find what you want to use and make sure you have the subscription or account set up before the class.
- Play with the program yourself. You want to make sure you know the ins and outs before you use it. Sure, students might teach you a few things during class, but you want to make sure you have a solid base, so you know how to operate it before the lesson starts.
- You might have to prep an example or two before you do this in class. Make sure you have saved any examples before class.
- You might also have to write out directions! Especially if you are looking to do this during centers. Written instructions will help students quickly start exploring the activity.
- Before each class, make sure the activities run well on your computer and interact correctly with your board.
- You might need to preload each activity to make sure that it works properly during class, and the Internet doesn't interfere with game time.
- Test your sound to make sure it is at a reasonable level for all students to hear!

During Class
- For an activity like Note and Rest Grab in Quaver, have students divide up into two teams.
  - Have each team line up on either side of the board.

FIGURE 4.5 Students enjoying an interactive game on the board (Photo Credit C. Dwinal)

- o Choose which team goes first. The first student steps up to the board and clicks Start. They answer the first question and then quickly step out of the way and head to the back of the line. While they do this, the next student in front steps up and answers the next question. This activity continues until the 30 seconds are up.
- o After the first team has gone, the second team now has its turn and follows the same directions as the first. The teams keeps answering questions until time runs out. The winner is the team with the highest score.
- o A variation on this is Quaver's Staff Champion, where you can choose the level of difficulty for students, from naming lines and spaces, to identifying notes on the full grand staff. Have the same format for students to compete against each other. Highest score wins!
- Try a pitch challenge using Blob Chorus.
  - o To start, bring up the Blob Chorus website and as a group, have the class answer as many questions correctly as they can. You can even have classes compete against each other. Write each class score on the board and the one with the highest score wins.
  - o A variation would be to plan this as a center station. Students can work in small groups to match pitch. Here are the directions:

- You have from now until it is time to switch centers. Click New Game and listen to all the little blobs sing their note, then listen carefully to the blob king as he sings his note. Click the little blob that matches the blob king's note the best. Continue to match the little blob's pitches to the blob king. When I give the warning to switch stations, write down your group number and score on the board. The group with the highest score will get to line up first when it is time to go back to class. If you need a little extra help, make sure to use one of the xylophones are at this station to help match pitch!

  o One other activity using this website is to bring out Boomwhackers, Orff instruments, or a piano. Click Play and have students listen carefully to each note the little blobs and blob king are singing. Have them match pitch and find the notes they are singing using the instruments that are available to them. Once they find the note pattern, the blobs are singing. Have the group write down the notes on the staff and play them together as one fluid melody.

- Get some cross-curricular connections going with StoryBots.com.
  o First, you will need to input a few pictures of your student's faces into the program before you do this activity. If you don't want to do all the students in class, add in the administrators and a few other teachers from the school.
  o During class, bring up StoryBots.com and click Books Starring You.
  o Select Orchestra Time and choose the individual that will be the star of the show. Read through the story and have students get engaged in the instruments of the orchestra. Do a recap about the instruments they saw in the book and learn about each one of them.
  o Another activity that you can do with Story Bots is to click on the Videos drop-down menu and select Starring You. There are several videos in there that are perfect quick movement break pieces. A couple of my favorites are "Chicken Bop," "The More We Get Together," and "Big Brown Boogieing Bear."

- Go to Teoria.com and select the Exercises section.
  o Turn up the sound so students will be able to hear the noises coming from the program.
  o Select the Chords and Triad training section.
  o Adjust the settings to make sure that each student in the class will get a turn while the class gets into a circle. You will be playing a big game of Around the World.
  o Click Play and have the first two students in the circle compete to see who can answer the question first. Whoever wins stands up behind the next student in the loop, and those two students will compete on the next question. If the student who is standing up wins, then they move on to the next student in the circle to contend

with. If the student who is sitting down wins, then the students switch places and the victor moves on to the next student.

o Continue the same procedure until you have gone entirely around the circle. The last student standing wins the game!

Assessment Tips:

- For an activity like Note and Rest Grab in QuaverMusic. Give it to students as a pretest, have students try to get their best score to submit to you in a 30-second period. Then administer it again after the completion of the unit to see if their scores improved.
- Bring up the Blob Chorus game and have the class try to answer as many questions as they can correctly. You can even do a round-robin and have each student answer one or two. A variation would be to give them a set of Boomwhackers and compete with another student to try to guess the answer by matching the pitch to the Boomwhacker first.
- Using the Teoria.com website, have students answer as many questions in the time allotted for that center. Have them report how many correct questions they answered before moving on to the next center.

How Does This Music Feel Activity

Recommended Grades: 1–6
Difficulty: Beginner
Time: 5–15 min.
Objective: Students will demonstrate proficiency in self-awareness by participating in the discussion.

Resources
- Computer
- Interactive board
- Speakers
- iTunes or YouTube
- Drawing app such as YouiDraw, SMART Notebook, ActivInspire software

This is a short and straightforward activity that promotes social and emotional learning while working on critical thinking skills. Sometimes you need to sit back, relax, and listen. When students walk in, especially after lunch or recess, they might need a few minutes to calm down. Or perhaps you've had a great class and want them to have a few minutes to rest. Turn on a piece of music and ask them to just listen and enjoy music for music's sake.

I have one lesson where I turn on an audio drama with Francis Scott Key talking about the night he wrote "The Star-Spangled Banner" from his point of view, and then I play the song itself. I turn out the lights and have them sit with their eyes closed to listen to it. Then we reflect on how Mr. Key might have felt that night, and how the song makes them feel. We then go into historical facts for that period and the birth of our country for added cross-curricular connections.

Before Class

- Acquire a piece of music you would like them to listen to and reflect on. Do not choose something too long to keep their engagement. It can be a classical piece or any other genre that you prefer. It could be fun to pick a piece that made an impact on current music today, such as something from the British Invasion or the disco era. I recommend either finding the song on YouTube or downloading it through iTunes or the Google Play Store (or another service). Downloading it as an MP3 would cut out the need to worry about any Wi-Fi issues that you might have on the day of the lesson.

- You most likely will want to give them some background on the piece. Do your research ahead of time to provide students with a little history lesson before the activity. For example, if you want to play a song from the Beatles, present a little background about the band and the impact that they made on American music culture. You could even bring up their first concert in the States on a video sharing service.

- Find a background to project on the board that reflects the piece of music you are listening to. It could be something related to the song, or a relaxing picture that promotes serenity and deep thinking.

- Before each class, cue up the piece of music you would like them to listen to. It could be something you have found on YouTube or purchased through iTunes.

- Check your interactivity on the board. You might need to recalibrate if the mouse is not clicking on the right area. The drawing tools require the board to be pretty accurate to create a legible document. If you are controlling the music or showing any videos or websites that relate to the piece of music, you will need to make sure that they are functional.

- Make sure the drawing function on your board is working and write a prompt on there for students to answer. Some examples could include:
  - How does this music make you feel?
  - Close your eyes and listen. What picture does this music bring to your mind?
  - What do you think the composer was trying to say with this music?
  - How do you think this music impacted our current music culture?
  - Can you relate to this music in any way? Is there someone at home that can relate to it?

During Class

- Bring students together and give them a little history about the piece of music. Tell them the story behind it and maybe a bit of the composer. Go over the prompt you would like them to answer.
  - Have them get comfy and start playing the music. The students can close their eyes, and you can turn out the lights. Tell them to take a few minutes to listen and, if the pen is free, to come up and write their answer to the prompt.
  - When everyone has had a turn, turn off the piece and discuss. Save the answers to the prompt to track student growth in their responses to music.
- Bring students together and pass out writing materials or have them take out their devices to do this activity. The goal for this activity is to write a paragraph reflection on the music.
  - Introduce the piece of music to the students. Introduce the composer to them and give them any historical background information on the piece that you would feel would be appropriate to share.
  - Give them this prompt: "Listen to this piece and describe any emotion that it creates inside of you. What picture do you think the composer is trying to convey? How do you think this piece of music has impacted our current culture?"
  - Have them spread out and get comfy.
  - Turn on the music and play it all the way through. Let them start writing. You might want to play through the piece one or two more times. Then allow them to finish writing.
  - Have a discussion regarding their thoughts about the piece!

Assessment Tip: Use the reflections students compose about the piece they listen to gauge their self-awareness and listening skills.

Incredibox

Recommended Grades: 2–6
Difficulty: Beginner
Time: 5–15 min.
Objective: Students will explore and show proficiency in vocal ostinatos by creating a short beatboxing piece and performing it for their classmates.

Resources

- Computer
- Interactive board
- Speakers

- Incredibox.com
- Individual devices

This activity means a lot to me. I have a unit in two different grade levels that use this recommended tool a lot. We do this activity in second grade when working on ostinatos (vocal and instrumental). The group gets together and explores how different musicians can create different sound patterns with their mouths. Then they build different combinations of the little guys on the screen using the Incredibox tool to see how the sequences would work together. Students then work in small groups to create their combinations and then compose their vocal ostinatos, which they then perform for the group. The students love it and put their all into it because it allows them to incorporate their current musical tastes. In the fifth-grade class I pull out Incredibox again and have them create and record compositions on individual devices. Some students send a copy to their parent or family member's email address. It is very refreshing to receive parents' emails within minutes, saying how amazed they were with their child's work and how much it meant to them to get a little brightness like that in the middle of their day. Something as simple as sharing music turns into a meaningful experience for the community.

Before Class
- Make sure Incredibox is accessible from your computer and works with your interactive board.
- The first few versions of Incredibox are Flash-enabled. If you want to use one of those make sure that it works with your interactive board. If not, you will need to use a wireless mouse to move the sounds around.
- If you are concerned with the characters in the program not having shirts on, use version 1, which has white t-shirts on them before you dress them up. I always used the later versions but told my students "They've got pajama bottoms on. We are helping to get them ready for school."
- If you want to have students do this as independent or small group work, then you will need individual devices. (Laptops are required for versions 1 through 4 since they are Flash enabled; versions 5 and up will need an iPad, as there is an app that needs to be downloaded to use the program.)
- Before each class, make sure Incredibox is up and running before students enter the class. It can be a Wi-Fi-heavy program at times, if you find that things run a little slow, close unnecessary tabs on your browser and any other programs that might be running.
- Check your interactivity on the board. You might need to recalibrate if the mouse is not clicking on the right area. Incredibox requires the calibration to be very accurate so the sounds coincide with the singers' movements.
- If you need to rent individual devices, make sure to get them before class starts. If you are a 1:1 school, then remind students to bring their devices to class this day.

During Class

- Have students come in and sit around the board. Put one character up to play the loop while students listen. After a minute, ask them what the character is doing. What is it called?
    - Introduce what an ostinato is and explain that the character on the screen is doing a vocal ostinato. Write out a rhythm on the board and have students repeat it a few times until they start getting it into their heads.
    - Write a couple more ostinatos on the board and have students use body percussion to play them. If they get proficient, add in a few more layers. Create a melody ostinato to go on top and have students perform with their voices.
    - Discuss what beatboxing is and relate the two together. Beatboxers are pretty much creating ostinatos with their voices.
    - Have students get into small groups and hand out one device per group. Have them go to Incredibox.com and create a short accompaniment track, a quick vocal ostinato that they can do together as a group on top of the piece they created so that it will blend in all together.
    - Give each group 2 minutes to pull together a quick tune on the board and figure out a vocal ostinato to perform with it while you keep the rest of the class going with a short game. When the group is ready, have them play for the group. Repeat for each group until done. (Variation: Give each student one mobile device to create their Incredibox tune on, and every group gets 10 minutes to figure out their song and find someone who has a similar sound. Have them, partner up and create a performance together using both of their pieces.)
- Bring out the individual devices and give students 20 minutes to create and record their piece in Incredibox. Have them email it to you or a family member when it is complete!

Assessment Tip: Assess students on their proficiency of vocal ostinatos by their Incredibox composition and performance for their classmates.

Projecting Music to Play and Notate

Recommended Grades: 2–12
Difficulty: Beginner
Time: 5 min.–1 hr.
Objective: The class will demonstrate proficiency in reading music together as an ensemble.

Resources

- Computer

- Interactive board
- Speakers
- PDF Reader, Noteflight, Quaver

This is another simple but effective way to use such an elaborate system—and it makes it a more memorable experience for the students. Although it is always essential to have students learn to read from the page on the music stand, teaching them to look up from their music stands and at the conductor is equally as important. This activity is easier to do at the younger grade levels as they play in general music classroom ensembles, but you can certainly do it with older groups in the form of warm-ups and sight-reading exercises.

Before Class

- Pick out the music you want to project. If you make physical copies of pieces, you can scan them into your computer, save them in a folder on your desktop, and project from there (Warning: Sharing any digital copies of music with colleagues after they are scanned into the computer is not endorsed by this publication. The purpose of scanning pieces of music to your computer for this activity is for your rehearsal and in-class instructional use only.) You are most likely to find a scanner in your school at the copy machine. Most copy machines now have a digital scanning feature that allows you to save directly to a USB drive or email the document to yourself.
- Programs like Noteflight and Quaver have digital and interactive scores built in that you can access if you have subscriptions to those. Those do not require you having to scan a piece of music.
- If you are using a digital score viewer like forScore, make sure you have created an account and learned how to use it before you do this activity.
- Create some storage space to retrieve your music easily. There might be some instances where you need to get it ready in the middle of class, so you need to have it easily accessible.
- Before each class, Bring up the piece of music that you would like students to read from and if it is interactive, make sure that it is operating correctly with the board.
- Check your interactivity on the board. You might need to recalibrate if the mouse is not clicking on the right area. You want to be able to scroll when required and of course use the writing tools on your board to notate the correct measures.
- Make sure students who sit in the back of the room can see the board! In an activity like this, you need to do a little zooming in on the board, or you need to readjust the seating so students can see everything.

During Class

- Bring up Noteflight and start a new score.
  - You can do this yourself, or you can have the class do it together. Create a short melody or rhythm for them to play on instruments. This activity can be for band

instruments or general classroom instruments. Once the melody or rhythm is created, play it together as a group. You can also create small pieces ahead of time and open beforehand. You can use this as a warm-up or sight-reading exercise as the rehearsal starts. This would also be a great time to use it as a teaching visual for a music theory unit in the general music class.

- Another activity is to take one of your favorite pieces that you've turned into a PDF. Project it on the board and have students play the piece by looking at the screen. Bring a student volunteer up to the front if needed to point to the notes to help students follow along. This is a perfect activity for students who are in the middle of an instrument unit in a general music class, or for warm-ups in an ensemble rehearsal.
- Quaver has hundreds of interactive scores that automatically highlight. Choose the song you want students to play, such as a recorder tune. Hit Play, and then students can follow along while you walk around the class helping students who need a little extra assistance.

Assessment Tip: Assess your students on how they participate in the full ensemble activity. Pay attention to how they contribute to the activity, and if they run into any trouble playing their instruments with their classmates.

Centers

Recommended Grades: 3–7
Difficulty: Moderate
Time: 20 min.–1 hr.
Objective: The class will show knowledge of content through independent and small group discovery during center time.

Resources
- Computer
- Interactive board
- Speakers
- Popplet.com, Groovy Music, YouTube, MusicTheory.net

Center time can sometimes be feared by many music educators. A music teacher might, if you add up total class time, see a class of students 24 hours total per year at the elementary level. Middle and high school might have a bit more class time but still not even close to the time a general classroom teacher spends with students. Although they can be tough to plan, centers can reap a big reward if you take the time to do them. I set up four or five stations around the room that have different levels of difficulty, depending on the class and grade level. It takes about a week to do these centers with third through fifth grades. I see each class twice every week, so we can spend a little extra time at each center. If you only see your

FIGURE 4.6 My music center kit has everything I need for center time (Photo Credit C. Dwinal)

students once a week, make sure they get to all the centers within one class period. Centers can be a way to shake up a standard lesson time and completely differentiate instruction in a new and glorious way. My students always get excited when they walk in and see the room set up for centers. It is an opportunity to let students take control over their learning and give you as the teacher some time to be able to work with students one-on-one and also to do some assessments. While students are at each center, it allows me to do some pull-out time with specific students who might need a little extra help or if I need time to do a performance-based assessment with individual students. I also spend time going to a couple of centers just visiting with students, which helps me see their strengths and weaknesses.

Before Class

- To keep everything organized, I have a container filled with the essentials, which include everything from directions for each center typed out and laminated dry erase boards, iPads, and lots of manipulatives that I created for different games. My center container includes:
  o A wooden crate labeled Music Centers.
  o Dry erase board with dry-erase markers.
  o Chalkboards painted different colors so that I can write the center name every time we do a new center.

o Index cards with an index card holder. (These cards have the center directions on them and are laminated.) Every time I come up with a new center, I create a new card and store it here. That way, I can pull up the center again if I want to.

o Large file folder to store examples, scores, pictures, and any manipulatives needed.

o A soft foam ball, because you never know when you need one!

o Chalk for chalkboards.

o A big bucket of crayons for any art-related projects that I have planned.

o Different colored popsicle sticks that have notes and rests on one side and note names on the other.

o A volleyball with notes and rests on it for a few games that we did.

o K'Nex! You would be surprised how much we used these to build different projects.

o Group number signs that have magnets for the whiteboard. I use these to indicate what center each group is supposed to do.

o Lots of reading books! I have a vast collection of books for general music class lessons. I use different books for different centers. Sometimes I put a few student favorites out so that they can read and perform them again.

o I also keep three iPads in this bucket. Students can use them for anything from a GarageBand composition to a research project. They are useful not only for centers but many other things in my room.

o In addition to these things, I always plan a technology center involving the board.

• When you are getting ready to do these centers, make sure to test them out and that the activities you plan on doing for your technology centers work with your board and will be easy for students to manipulate in small groups. You might need to recalibrate the board before students come in. If you are doing a center that involves composition, you will especially need to make sure the board is calibrated for students to be able to drag the notes and rests onto it.

• I suggest typing up directions for each activity and laminating them for future use! You can put them into the index card holder, as indicated above.

• For Activity No. 1, you will need clipboards, paper, and pencil for each student. If you do not have clipboards, old textbooks will work as well, or you might have a colleague who has a basket of clipboards that they can loan you.

• For Activity No. 2, you will need a mobile device for students to record work. I have a couple of iPads that stay in my room. If you do not have one, ask your technology department to borrow one for this activity.

• Activity No. 3 will require coloring materials along with some paper. Make friends with your art teacher to get supplies!

• Activity No. 4 will require index cards with writing utensils.

o Also, remember to put everything you need for each center in an organized folder or bucket. You won't need much for the centers in these specific activities, but if you are looking to expand your centers, you'll need to look into options such as expandable file folders, sealed buckets, or wooden crates as mentioned earlier.

- Before each class, bring up the activity you would like for the center and leave out the instructions in a place for all students to see.
- Set out the necessary materials for the activity.
- Check your sound! You want to make sure the levels are suitable for small group activity.
- When students enter the room, have them sit down in their usual area and not near the centers. Go over rules of the centers and set expectations for each. Divide the students into groups and then assign them each to a center and have them get going!

During Class

- Activity No. 1 will use Popplet.com, which is a mind mapping tool that allows students to organize their thoughts into a cool-looking web. For this, we'll assume students have been learning about the topic of country music, but you may want to choose a different theme for them to map out.
  - Instructions for the students are as follows: You have been learning about country music for the past few classes. For this activity, please work as a group and map out all the facts about the topic that you can. Start with the word "country" at the center and expand your web to talk about artists that made country music what it is, typical instruments artists use, venues that are famous for the genre, etc.
- Activity No. 2 will require a mobile device to have students record themselves as they make their way through GroovyMusic.com and create their work as they go.
  - Instructions: Using Groovy Jungle, create a masterpiece as a group by places the parts of the jungle on different areas of the screen. Once you have created your music, talk as a group, and make at least two changes that you feel would make the music better. Then turn on the video recorder and record yourselves answering the question, "What do you think about the music we made?"
- Activity No. 3 uses YouTube to play the classical piece of music "Danse Macabre" by Saint-Saens. There are many versions of this on the site but my favorite version to play is: https://www.youtube.com/watch?v=YyknBTm_YyM. Make sure you set out plenty of coloring tools to let the students use their imaginations!
  - Instructions: Take one piece of plain white paper and fold it into quarters. Draw footsteps in one corner, a violin in the other, a skeleton or skull in another corner, and ghosts in the last. Play the music on the board and listen carefully. Every time you hear a section that sounds like dancing or a waltz, draw a mark in the footstep corner of the page, when you hear violins playing draw a mark in the violin corner. When students hear the marimbas they put a mark in the skeleton corner and when they hear music that sounds haunting like a ghost they put it in the ghost corner of the page. Compare with your group after the song is done to see how much each of you heard!

- Activity No. 4 is best for older students. It uses the Key Signature Identification tool on MusicTheory.net and note cards.
  - Instructions: Take a small stack of notecards and a pen or pencil. One at a time, each person in your group takes a turn answering one of the questions on the board. Everyone in the group must write down the key signature on one side of their index card and write down the correct answer on the other when your time is complete. At the end, you should have a stack of study cards to help you better learn your key signatures!

Assessment Tip: Centers are the best time for you as the educator to spend more one-on-one time with students. Use the center time to meet with individual students to assess them on specific topics from the ones the centers are about to other concepts you may be working on in class. Take your time to do assessments during centers.

Interactive Storytelling

Recommended Grades: 3–10
Difficulty: Expert
Time: 25 min.–2 class periods
Objective: Students will show an understanding of a piece of music by creating a digital story about the musical selection.

Resources
- Computer
- Interactive board
- Speakers
- Storybird.com or Book Creator app
- Individual devices

I'm a sucker for a good story. If I can add music to it, even better! We create stories all the time in my class, from story circles that are based around certain characters, to taking books like The Little Old Lady Who Was Not Afraid of Anything *and creating a musical story-scape around that book. We then move on to more significant pieces of music and create stories based on them. This progression includes literacy in every step. Music always tells a story, and when you point it out to a student, it makes a larger impact on them.*

Before Class
- Create a teacher account on Storybird.com. You can have students create their accounts in class, then work on their assignments independently.
- The goal of this activity is to create a story based on a classical piece of music. Students can get creative and do something entirely "outside the box," or write a story that attempts to reflect what the composer was trying to get across.

- Choose two pieces of music for students to write a story around: one to do together as a class and one for students to do individually. I would recommend having these in MP3 form for this activity. Some examples of songs you could use:
  - *The Four Seasons* by Vivaldi
  - *The Nutcracker* by Tchaikovsky
  - *The Planets* by Holst
  - "In the Hall of the Mountain King" by Grieg
- You as the teacher might want to create a story first to show as an example.
- After you have created an example, you can create an assignment to give to the students in your Storybird.com teacher resources.
- Before each class, make sure that the site loads on your computer.
- Check your interactivity with the board. You might need to recalibrate if the mouse is not clicking on the right area. These writing programs require the board to be very accurate when using them to make things more legible for the work you are doing.
- Start by cueing up the songs you want the students to listen to for their stories. If you are playing the song through a cloud-based streaming program, play it through all the way to make sure it is loaded for class and will not skip due to Wi-Fi connection errors.
- You will need to have students bring individual devices to class if you are a 1:1 school. If you have rentable devices or a computer lab you can reserve them before class instead. If you do not have device access, prepare a pencil and a short stack of paper for students to make a book. To make a book, take a short stack of blank copy paper, fold it in half, then staple the folded part to create the book binding.

During Class

- Play the music of choice for the students; ask them to close their eyes and imagine what is going on while the music plays. Is there a story that they are seeing? What do they think the composer was trying to tell their audience? Discuss with the class how a piece of music, even without words, can still tell the story, whether it be a specific one that the composer wrote for the piece or one that the audience can imagine themselves.
- Come up with ideas for a story that could be playing out as the piece plays. Does it spark a different creative bug instead, or is there a specific story that this music is telling you? Brainstorm a short list of stories with students and write them on your board. You either choose one that would be best or have students do a quick vote.
- As a group, type out a short story together based on the music and the topic that was chosen. Type it out first before moving to the Storybird website.
- Bring up Storybird.com and have students look at your example so they know how it should look.
- Transfer the group story to a Storybird.com website and have students help you chose the theme and pictures to go along with the story.
- Read through the book together and have the piece of music playing in the background softly as you read. Ask students whether the story they created together works with the music. If they say yes, then ask why? If no, what could we change?

- Tell students the goal of the next activity is to have them write their own story using a different piece of music. Example goals for this activity could be:
  - Listen to the music that was chosen for this activity and write down any notes that might help you remember what went on in the piece and any ideas that you may have had for the story while you were listening.
  - Brainstorm ideas for a topic of a story you could write based on the song that you are listening to. Write down all you can think of before narrowing it down to the best idea.
  - Create an outline of the story, just a summary of what the beginning, middle, and end will be, then fill each section with what will go between scenes.
  - Write your story down. Make it as clear and detailed as possible.
  - Head to Storybird.com and start pulling the book together based on the story that you wrote; choose a great theme, and add lots of pictures for the story.
  - Read through it while you have the piece of music playing in the background. Do the music and story work together? If not, what do you need to change music and to make it work?
- Project the goals on the board for students to have always at hand as they work on this project.
- Have students go to Storybird.com on their own devices (or use pencil and paper) and go to the class account you made to see the assignment.
- Give them a refresher on how to create their own stories using Storybird.com.
- Play the second piece of music. Give students time to brainstorm and respond to the selection. Then have them write out a basic outline for the story before they move on to the book creator.
- Have students create their own story with words, audio, and visuals and submit their assignment to you.
- Have some volunteers come up to the board to show their creations and read their works of art.
- When everyone has completed their books, send some out to the school community after you have received permission to share. Make sure to be available for story time in other classes if needed!

Assessment Tip: Assess students on their final storybook product. Pay close attention to the music that they have chosen for the story and how it relates to the music.

Creating Accompaniment Tracks

Recommended Grades: 3–12
Difficulty: Moderate
Time: 10 min.–1 hr.

Objective: The class will show knowledge of form and song construction by creating pieces of music together by digital means.

Resources

- Computer
- Interactive board
- Speakers
- QuaverMusic's QGrooves or GarageBand.

Sometimes we create beats together for just the sake of making music and getting creative. The most basic form of creating music is to let students explore and create on their own with little to no restrictions. It allows students to take control and encourages them to make more in-depth songs with more advanced tools. Making music with minimum requirements takes a lot of stress off of the students and lets their creativity go wild. After they come up with a piece, we chat about it: Should we change anything? Should we add? Is this the best we can make it? Maybe we add a chant or rap over it, then throw in some rhythm sticks. We always have a ball! With one of my fifth-grade classes, we composed a rhythm together on the board that fit the melody and beat to a song we composed on GarageBand. Then we added another accompaniment track for some extra flavor!

Before Class

- Make sure you can pull up the creative tool that you want to work with for this activity. I suggested QGrooves or GarageBand because they are tools that involve sequencing loops of premade music, which makes it a little easier to create a full piece of music in a shorter amount of time. This activity is great to use a few weeks into a songwriting unit to encourage students to keep learning about writing more advanced pieces and diving deeper into more traditional composition. If you do this at a different time or have a different levels of students, you might want to use traditional notation or a completely different creation tool. It's up to you!
- If you need to create accounts or download anything, do it before you start using it with students. For downloads, get together with your technology department to make sure that the right programs have been pushed out to all the student devices. When it comes to creating accounts for students, you could meet up with your tech department, or work with the company that created the software. You could also create just a few accounts for all the students to periodically share depending on your class situation. These will come in handy for this activity and beyond as you continue throughout the year. This is a set-it-and-forget-it sort of task!
- Before each class, pull up the creative tool and make sure it is in working order before the students enter. If you need to add any notes or loops to get the students

started, make sure you have that up to prevent any hang-up time during class. Adding different notes and rests will add in another challenge to students as they create their music.

During Class

- Pull up the creative tool and play the "One-line-at-a-time story game." The students sit in a circle and one at a time each comes up and adds one section to the piece until everyone has taken a turn, and there is a full piece of music. You could also have a student lead this activity, directing students to come up to the board. Students can also help each other with technical difficulties.
  - o Give the group either a time limit or a measure limit so that way they are not going on forever. Remind them that this is like a story and should have a beginning, a middle, and something that sounds like an end.
  - o Edits to the song should be agreed upon by the whole class if they need to be changed. The fun about a full class activity like this is celebrating the creative choices by all students, whether they are bold choices or not.
- Another activity starts with breaking up the class into two groups. Have the first team come up and create a short four-measure composition using the creative tool you have chosen. The next team can either use their turn to make one change to the other team's composition, or add four measures of their own. Then the next group can do the same. Teams can only make one change every other turn to allow for the composition to move forward and not going back and forth over one section of the piece. Teams also cannot go back and make another change to a previous part of the composition once it has been changed!
- The next activity is about building ensemble skills.
  - o Have the class compose an accompaniment track together using a creative tool of your choice. This activity will work better with a track composed with a loop generator like QGrooves from Quaver, or GarageBand.
  - o After the class has created an accompaniment track, have them work on a melodic or rhythmic ostinato, depending on what instruments you would like students to use. Or you could do both!
  - o Break out the Orff instruments if you have created a melody and take out a drum if you have created a rhythm together. Practice everything together as a full ensemble.
  - o For a little added effect, add in a rap or a choreographed dance!

Assessment Tip: Give each student or group a specific form they must follow in their creation. Once they have created their piece, have them share it with their classmates, and be sure to explain the form they followed. Assess them on how well they followed the form in their creation.

Composing Pieces on Noteflight

Recommended Grades: 3–12
Difficulty: Beginner
Time: 10 min.–1 hr.
Objective: The class will demonstrate knowledge of basic music theory through compositional activities with the Noteflight program.

Resources

- Computer
- Interactive board
- Speakers
- Noteflight

What about composing as a class? Write a full piece of music with your students that they can immediately hear, think about, make changes, and then be able to play it on instruments. When I first started teaching, we did a lot of composition activities where I would bring up a tool, and then together we would compose a piece. As we went along, I would be able to interject different tips and tidbits about the notes and rests they were putting into the composition. It is an activity that allows me to talk with students about music theory while creating a visual about what they are learning. We can then use this final product for composition pen pals, assessments, or to display to the school community as a show of what we are learning.

Before Class

- If you need to create accounts or download anything, do it before you start using it with students. Compositional tools like Quaver and Noteflight require a subscription with a username and password. Software such as Finale Notepad will ask you to download it to your computer. Make sure you have set up any accounts before you start this activity.
- Make sure your sound is working! One of the benefits of using notation software is the feedback it provides. Make sure students can hear what it is playing!
- Play with the software yourself. You want to make sure you know the ins and outs of what you are going to use before you use it with students.
- You might want to create a few examples yourself of the kinds of compositions you want the classes to achieve. Write out a couple so they can visually see the expectations and save them in your files to bring up as you are explaining the activity.
- You can also create a few fill-in-the-blank compositions that will help students get going when they are composing. Make sure to create those before you do this activity with classes.

- Before each class, pull up the creative tool and make sure it is in working order before the students enter. If you need to open up any examples or fill-in-the-blank activities for students for this activity, make sure you have that up to prevent any hang-up time during class.
- Test your sound to make sure it is at a reasonable level for all students to hear the notes that are playing!
- Check your interactivity on the board. You might need to recalibrate if the mouse is not clicking on the right area. These notation programs require the board to be very accurate when using them.

During Class

- Pull up the creative and play the "One-line-at-a-time story game."
  - The students sit in a circle and one at a time each comes up and adds one section at a time to the piece. It can be one measure, one phrase, or even just one note. Have them explain their thought process about their choices out loud for the class.
  - Go until your time limit is up or you feel there is a finished piece of music in front of you.
  - Play the piece for the class. Have students listen to each other's parts and see if they flow together and sound like a cohesive piece of music. Ask the group if there is anything they would like to go back and change. Have them brainstorm and be very specific which parts (down to the intervals and different notes), then circle them using your board's drawing tools. Then go back and discuss each place and come up with a solution on how to fix it.
  - After you have gone back and edited the piece, play it from start to finish, so the students hear everything. Ask students to come up with one word to describe the music as a whole. Instruct them not to use vague words like good, bad, okay, or meh. This activity will help them practice critical thinking skills as they come up with more sophisticated ways to describe the music that they have created.
- For this activity, you will need to break up the class into groups of three or four students.
  - Give each group 5 minutes to talk about how they will compose a short piece of music. Have them designate someone as the person who puts the notes on the board, someone who will help each person in the group have a turn, and one person who will make sure that the measures meet the requirements for their mini composition.
  - Have the first team come up and create their short four-measure composition using the creative tool that you have chosen. Ask that it includes at least three types of notes and rests that they have been learning. If it is a melody, ask that it has an excellent melodic contour and that the group can perform it if requested.
  - Once the first team has its turn, ask the next group to come up and add four measures of their own. Then the next team can do the same. Repeat until every team has had a turn.

- o After everyone has had a turn at the board, play the whole thing together. Ask students to focus primarily on the transitions between each group's mini-composition. Do they sound like they go along? If not, could you compose one measure between each to fix the contour and bring it back to a piece that sounds like one person wrote it?
- o Assign each group one additional measure between each other's four-measure compositions that will connect each of the pieces. Have the groups come up one by one to put up their extra measure.
- o Listen to the whole piece together; start a discussion on the reflection of the selection as a whole. Does anything need to be edited? As a class, make the edits together.
- o Then, arrange the piece. Take out the instruments and practice the parts piece by piece as a class and perform it together!
- Have the class compose a rhythm together.
  - o Get out either dry erase boards and markers or paper and pencils and pass out to each student. Give each student their number that corresponds to a measure.
  - o Instruct students to create one measure of rhythm in 4/4 time using at least two types of notes and rests. Ask students to make sure that they create a rhythm that they can perform themselves.
  - o When the students complete the task, ask them to fill in the measure that they were assigned with the rhythm that they created, while they waiting for others to finish. Have them bring out a drum and transfer their rhythm to an it.
  - o When everyone is done, play the whole thing together and have students listen to everything together. Transfer the entire piece over to percussion and perform it together as a class.
  - o After the class composes the whole rhythm and can play it on the class percussion, add a melody line together as a class to play Orff instruments. Pass out instruments and practice and play the melody line together as an ensemble. Then take out a few students who will play the rhythmic line on drums as the rest of the class plays the melody line.
  - o If you have a little extra time and some motivated students, add in rap, or a choreographed dance!

Assessment Tips:

- Assess students on their participation in the story activity. Pay close attention to their contribution to the piece.
- Have the student perform the music that they created for their classmates. Assess them on how they played and their composition as a whole.

Create Your Story Music

Recommended Grades: 3–12
Difficulty: Moderate
Time: 10 min.–1 hr.
Objective: Students will demonstrate proficiency of found sounds by choosing sounds that are reflective of a story and how they perform it for their classmates.

Resources
- Computer
- Interactive board
- Speakers
- Kids story, examples can be *Click, Clack, Boo, The Little Old Lady Who Was Not Afraid of Anything*, etc.
- Drawing app such as YouiDraw, SMART Notebook, ActivInspire software
- Musical instruments

I originally picked up this activity from my co-op teacher while student teaching. We took the book The Little Old Lady Who Was Not Afraid of Anything *and turned it into a piece of music. That book lends itself to certain points where students can play instruments to enhance the story and make it more interactive. Other books do the same or allow students to build music behind the story for example,* Skeleton Cat *and* Pete the Cat. *Music and stories go so well together. Integrating books this way is an excellent approach to promoting literacy and music!*

Before Class
- Acquire the books you would like to use with this activity.
- Make sure you have drawing capabilities on your interactive board.
- Check your interactivity on the board. You might need to recalibrate if the mouse is not clicking on the right area. These drawing programs require the board to be very accurate.
- Collect all the instruments you will want to have available for students. I have a box of auxiliary percussion and a selection of portable Orff instruments that students were able to choose from when creating these story soundscapes and compositions.
- Before each class, bring up your drawing tool on the board.
- Set out the instruments for students to use during the activity. I place them out on tables in a buffet-style spread that allows students to view and choose their instruments quickly.

During Class
- Bring students into the room and be sure they pass the instrument buffet table, so they get a beautiful view of the selection of instruments that they can choose.

FIGURE 4.7 Students get creative with their instruments (Photo Credit C. Dwinal)

- Start to read the book of choice to the students. For this example, the text of choice is *The Little Old Lady Who Was Not Afraid of Anything*; there is time for playing instruments after every addition to the jack-o'-lantern. The book puts the sounds that need to be matched to an instrument into italics.
  - Ask students to identify what instrument goes with which sounds. Write them out on the board. Then with the help of the students, write out the rhythms for each instrument, and practice them.
  - Pass out those instruments to specific students.
  - Reread the story and have students play those specific instruments during those points in the story to make a musical piece!
- A variation on the first activity can be to read the book of choice to the students. Specifically, for *The Little Old Lady Who Was Not Afraid of Anything*, there is time for playing instruments after every addition to the jack-o'-lantern.
  - The goal of this activity will be to add a musical track to the book. Student instructions for this project:
    - Get together with your group and pair a musical instrument with each part in the story that asks for it (after every section, look for the italicized words). Write down which instrument will go with each part.

- Assign each member from your group a role to play. If you have more members than parts, have a few people double up.
- Come up with a little rhythm to play on your instrument when your teacher reads the book to your group, and it is your instrument's turn in the story.
- Write that rhythm down using your device or pencil and paper provided.
- Practice with your group until it is your turn to perform for the class!
  - Get students into groups and have them brainstorm what instruments to use and who will be playing what instrument. Pass out pencils and paper so they can write it down. Or if they have devices have them use a note-taking app.
  - Ask students to write out what the rhythms for each part will be, get the instruments, and practice. They can either write it out on paper or use their devices.
  - When they are ready, have each group come up and write their music on the board and then play their parts as you reread the story to the class.
    - Use the interactive board as a place to share what instruments will go with each sound. For a template, you could have the bullet points below repeated for the number of sounds that you need for this activity.
    - Sound
    - Instrument
    - Rhythm

Assessment Tip: Assess each group on how they perform their piece for the class. Focus primarily on their instrument choices and rhythms that they created for each part. You can also assess each group on how well they work together.

Composer Research

Recommended Grades: 4–12
Difficulty: Moderate
Time: 1 to 2 class periods
Objective: Students will give an oral presentation using digital visuals to demonstrate knowledge of a chosen musical composer to the class.

Resources
- Computer
- Interactive board
- Speakers
- Google search engine
- Google Slides, Glogster, Prezi, Keynote
- Individual devices

FIGURE 4.8 Sometimes I decorate with these for a little extra inspiration (Photo Credit C. Dwinal)

One of the best things that you can give to a student in their education is a sense of pride and ownership over what they are learning. Giving them a mission and then guiding them toward the finish line can be a simple activity that enhances the learning environment above and beyond just a straightforward lecture style. We as music educators can do this easily, especially when diving into topics such as musical genres and composers. When it comes to composers, you might be able to only cover a few during your instruction, but if you leave it to the students, they can dive into more of them than you might have ever thought to introduce to them before. I do this with my older students. It is a project that we do at the end of a unit for them to show learned knowledge of what we focused on. I rent out devices for a couple of class periods and build a goal sheet. Depending on the class, students are either assigned a composer, or they chose one themselves. Then they are sent on their way to work while I wander around the room making sure the students are on task. When they complete their work, they give a short presentation to their peers about their composer. It helps build public speaking skills.

Before Class

- Make sure students have access to the presentation tool of your choice. There are many options out there beyond Google Slides, Glogster, and Prezi. You need to make sure that if they need accounts you create them before class. If you are a Google School, then you should have immediate access to Google Slides. Sites like Glogster and Prezi will require an account to save the work.

- If you are going to do this with younger students come up with a list of kid-safe websites your classes can use to research. You can create a custom search engine through Google, which will allow you to set only certain websites for the search engine to pull from when students are researching their composers. There are several kid-friendly search engines including:
  - o Kidtopia.info
  - o Kidrex.org
  - o Kiddle.co
  - o SafeSearchKids.com
- Make sure you have done at least a few lessons on composers or musical periods to give your students some prior knowledge of the subject.
- Put together a list of all the composers that students will choose from in this project. You might want to narrow it down to a particular musical period or a specific style of musical composer. There are plenty of composers so every one of your students should be able to have a different one.
- Create a goal list for your students to be able to use when they are doing this project. This list would be something you could also project onto the board as they are working to remind them of what they need to do. Here is an example of a list of goals to give to each student:
  - o Find out who your composer is and research how to pronounce their name correctly!
  - o Get out an individual device and open up the notes program on it. Make sure to type out your full name, homeroom class, and the name of your composer at the top.
  - o Open up an Internet browser and go to the search engine. Find at least four reputable sites that give you useful information on your composer and write them down in your notes.
  - o Go back to the websites that you chose and find ten reliable and useful facts about your composer. Make sure that you write down all of the research you find into your notes.
  - o Open Google Slides.
  - o Take all of the facts that you wrote down and create a 3-minute presentation about your composer that you will present to the class at the end of this project.
  - o Make sure to include some interesting facts about their life, essential pieces of music that they gave to the world, and any strange quirks that they might have had. Add pictures, videos, and audio clips in your presentation that will help support the facts that you found!
  - o Sign up for a presentation slot for show day!

- Before each class, make sure your Wi-Fi is running correctly. Also, make sure that students can have easy access to the interactive board when it comes time to present their findings.
- Check your sound! You want to make sure the levels are suitable for presentation time.
- Make sure students have access to mobile devices. If you are a 1:1 school, this project will be easier to start. If you need to rent out machines, you will need to make sure that you assign each student a specific device so they can go back and find their work on it in the next class period.
- Have copies of the goal checklist ready for students to take while they are working, and have a projectable version on the board.

During Class

- Students should have prior knowledge of composers before doing this activity. This project would be a perfect ending to a unit as a final assessment to show what they learned. It also demonstrates the students' skills in researching and communicating information.
- Bring students together and discuss the project that they will be doing for the next couple of classes. The main objectives are:
  ○ Find a composer to research about.
  ○ Write down four websites in which you will find the research.
  ○ Write down ten facts about the composer.
  ○ Collect pictures, videos, and audio clips about the composer.
  ○ Create a short 3-minute presentation with slides that you will present to the class.
  ○ Sign up for a presentation slot.
  ○ Give your presentation on the composer you were assigned!
- Set rules for the next few class periods to create a calm space for working on projects. Some examples of best practices can be:
  ○ Treat your devices with the same respect as you would in any other class. Make sure to keep them squarely on the floor or a table when you are using them!
  ○ Keep the noise level down. You are all working by yourselves, so noise should be at a minimum.
  ○ Leave your computer at your desk and come up to me if you have any questions or problems.
  ○ When you have completed your slideshow, save it and email it to me for your presentation.
  ○ If you have completed the task before others, practice your presentation!
- Pass out the goal checklist as well as the composer that they will be focusing on for this project. Have students get their devices and find their spot in the room to get going.
- Project the goals right on the board so they can see them any time from any part of the room. Make sure that you move around the room to help students through the project.

- Using their mobile devices, students will find at least ten facts about the composer which include
  - o Anything unusual about their backstory and personal life
  - o Their most famous pieces
  - o The most exciting things about their career.
- Students will put together an interactive 3-minute presentation about their composer using pictures, videos, and audio clips in their slideshow.
- Students will make sure to sign up for a slot on presentation day.
- On presentation day, students will use the interactive board to display their presentation. (It is best to have them either put it in a shared folder that you can access or email their presentations to you before show day.)
- After everyone has completed their presentations, reflect on the experience together, and compile everyone's submissions into one big display that you can share with the administration and others in the school community.

Assessment Tip: Assess students on their final submission. Pay close attention to the content of their presentations.

Exit Tickets

Recommended Grades: 4–12
Difficulty: Beginner
Time: 5–35 min.
Objective: Students will demonstrate knowledge learned during the day's lesson by submitting an exit ticket before they leave class.

Resources
- Computer
- Interactive board
- Speakers
- Google Forms
- PollEverywhere.com or Kahoot.it

Being in the music room, I only see students for a short time each year, which makes it hard to know whether they are grasping the concepts that I am teaching them on a weekly or daily basis. What comes in handy for me are exit tickets, short questions that students answer at the end of a unit or right before they exit the classroom. Exit tickets come in many forms. I've seen teachers use other methods, from actual cards that students use to write their answers, to call-and-response vocal games that a student has to complete before they can line up. I have even had a friend of mine create a Yes or No touchpad from a Makey Makey kit where

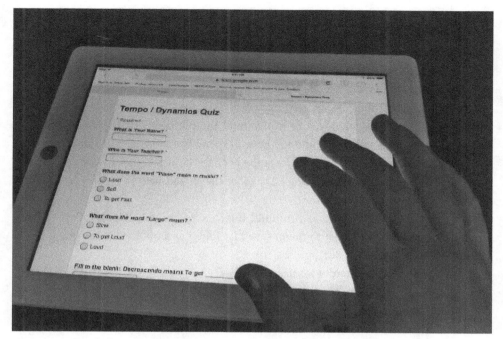

FIGURE 4.9 Google Forms on the iPad make quick assessments easy (Photo Credit C. Dwinal)

students were able to answer the question by touching their answer on the pad as they exited the room. Exit tickets do not necessarily need to have a student's name attached but can act as a poll to better help collect student data. I usually go the Google Forms route for my exit tickets because I collect student names with their answers to better know who needs a little more help, or whether I need another class period to explain the topic to everyone. I usually have an activity going in another part of the room and call one person to the board at a time to type their answers. I can also do a quick anonymous poll on their devices.

Before Class
- Make sure you have the proper software on your interactive board, and it has the newest updates. Google is a resource that requires an updated system and memory to run.
- Check the interactivity on your board. You might need to recalibrate if the mouse is not clicking on the right area. Programs like Google Forms require a calibrated board to run because students will be typing or selecting answers on it.
- Get access to Google and Google Drive. This way, you can start creating forms and other documents. If you are a Google School, you should have access to all of the Google tools.
- Practice with the program before you use it. You will need to be comfortable with it during class time! Google Forms might require some help from others to get acquainted

with it. Talk to your tech coach or a coworker with a knack for technology if you need someone to help walk you through how to make a form.

- You will need to set up your forms before you use them with students. Each one of them will come with a spreadsheet that will log all answers. Make sure that:
  - The first question will need to be short-answer open-ended, where students can put their names in.
  - Try to keep the questions to one or two total and preferably multiple-choice questions. Each student should not have to spend more than 2 to 3 minutes at the board, answering questions before going back to the activity they were doing.
  - Know where to go in your Google Drive for the spreadsheet (it will be the same name as the form you created).
- Save any exit ticket forms that you build into one file in your Google Drive. If you need a quick shortcut to get to them, save that folder as a bookmark to your Internet browser for quick access during class.
- If you decide to go a different route:
  - Go to PollEverywhere.com and create the poll that you are going to use during the next lesson. Made sure to test it with your device before trying it with students. If you are renting student devices for this activity, make sure to try it out on those devices before moving forward.
  - Type in Kahoot.com and create an account. Then start building your exit ticket quiz. You can try out the student side of the activity by heading to Kahoot.it on your device and playing the Kahoot quiz game to make sure that it works.
- Before each class, make sure the program is up and operational on your board. You will need to bring it up for the class you are about to see before they enter the room.

During Class

- Put the exit ticket Google Form on the board.
  - Go over with students what the questions are and how they are expected to answer.
  - Let students know that they will be coming up one at a time to answer on the board. They will need to listen for their name or know to watch for the person sitting next to them in the activity to come back before they go up to answer the question. They will need to be quick because they should already know the answers to the questions if they have been paying attention.
  - Have students do an activity like practicing a piece of music they are working on individually, a quick composition activity, or maybe small group discussion. Quietly and quickly, students will come up to the board and fill in the form. To log their answers and make room for the next student, they will need to hit the Submit button and turn in new replies again. Their answers will be logged in the spreadsheet as soon as they hit Submit

- Look at the spreadsheet after every student in the class has completed it and left for the day. Discover the trends in answers to see if any student had some trouble answering. Keep a log of what you discover for next class. If you have too many that answered incorrectly, then you might need to have a review day at the next class period.
- Pull up PollEverywhere.com and bring up your poll for this class.
  - Have students bring out their devices or get them from the rented cart that you acquired before class started.
  - You can only present one question at a time to students. Bring up the poll and have them visit the website on the board to answer or text in their answers to each question as you paginate through them. After they answer each question, it will give you a graph of the answers look so you can quickly get an overview of where they are in their understanding of the topics you have been teaching in class.
  - Use the anonymous data you acquire to determine whether or not you can move onto the next topic or next step in the unit.
- Go to Kahoot.com and bring up your game for this class.
  - Have students bring out their devices or get them off the rented cart that you acquired before class.
  - You can only present one question at a time to students. As you bring up the website, have them visit the website Kahoot.it to answer each question as you bring them up. Students will be asked to put in a username or their real name to play the game. It is your choice as to what you ask them to put in the name field. The game will put up the top-scoring players based on whether or not they answered correctly and how fast they answered the question.
  - Give a prize to the top-scoring individual!
  - Use the data to determine a student's understanding of the topics in the quiz and whether they have comprehended the material you have taught in class.

Assessment Tip: Exit tickets are mini-assessments that demonstrate a student's understanding of the topic during the lesson that day. Assess students on their answers to their exit tickets and use them as a way to gauge if the class is getting the concepts you are teaching or if you need to backtrack or slow down for a bit.

World Music Presentation

Recommended Grades: 7–11
Difficulty: Expert
Time: 4 to 5 Class Periods
Objective: Students will demonstrate learned knowledge of their assigned country's music and culture by creating a final 3D product to present to the class.

Resources
- Computer
- Interactive board
- Speakers
- Google Slides
- CoSpaces Edu
- Audacity or GarageBand
- Individual devices
- Google Cardboard (Optional but fun)

This project can take learning and instruction to a whole new level. Allow students to use several resources and tailor a final product of their knowledge into something they are excited to present. Adopting a universal concept like learning about different cultures and their music (which can be completed in collaboration with other colleagues like your foreign language teachers) can lead to a memorable experience. When I had taken high school Spanish for several years, one of our big projects was to pick a country, create a presentation about its culture, and cook one of the most popular foods from that country. I remember I chose Jamaica, and I did extensive research on its music, food, language, and culture. Then I made a delicious dessert before putting my visuals together. Of course, I still remember a lot about that project, so it made an impact on my learning. This was many years ago; what if I had the technology that is available today? There are endless products now that students can use. I could have created a steel pan piece to play, then coded a VR experience of the steel pan to show to the class on the board or allowed them to explore a steel pan band playing in an actual venue in Jamaica. The possibilities have tripled since I was in school!

Before Class
- Make this a project to finish off a world music unit. That way, students have prior knowledge of different cultures from all over the globe.
- Make sure your interactive board is up and working and has the proper software installed. Also, check your interactivity with the board. You might need to recalibrate if the mouse is not clicking on the right area. VR programs require the board to be very accurate when using them to move things around and explore your board VR experience.
- If you do not have accounts set up to CoSpaces and Google, make sure to create accounts beforehand. CoSpacesEdu is free for the basic plan, but the Pro package does offer you more options.
- If you are not a 1:1 school make sure that you reserve either the computer lab or cart of devices beforehand (laptops are preferable when students make their creations).
- If you would like to have Google Cardboard accessible for students to use in their presentations, make sure you get some viewers for your students beforehand. If your

FIGURE 4.10 A student working hard on their project (Photo Credit C. Dwinal)

budget is tight to get them, places like DonorsChoose.org is an easy way to get inexpensive resources covered like these. Google sells these directly on their site. You could also collaborate with your art teacher to make your own. Google has directions on how to make these viewers here https://arvr.google.com/cardboard/manufacturers/

- Connect with your foreign language teachers and technology teachers. You could build in some great collaborative activities with a project like this that could make a big splash in the school culture. You could have them do the research, and create the presentations in your class, learn the language and culture in foreign language, and the technology teacher could work with them on their VR experience. Come together at the end for one big final event!

- Get familiar with the CoSpaces Edu program and create an example that you will show students later. The ultimate goal of this project is to create a scene that represents the music of their selected culture. It can be a famous venue or a 3D visual of an instrument that is special to the culture. Create one example for students and give them options to go further!

- Set down the goal and the activities they need to complete to get to that goal. Create a checklist in Google Docs and share it with the students.

- o Goal: Please create an interactive experience that demonstrates your knowledge of the music, language, food, and the history of the culture you selected.
  - Choose a country and research its music, including any instruments, folk songs, and dances unique to the country. Also study its primary language, food, and specific historical moments that are important to the culture.
  - Find at least one video on YouTube that demonstrates the music from the country.
  - Choose at least one traditional folk song that you will be recording for your presentation. Learn how to sing it and record it into either Audacity or GarageBand and edit it into an MP3.
  - Write a 500-word paper on your country describing all the research you have done about your country.
  - Create a minimum eight-slide presentation about your selected country. Make sure to include several pictures and the video you selected.
  - Using CoSpaces Edu, design and create an immersive VR experience that demonstrates your new knowledge of the country.
  - Present your project to the class.
- Before each class, make sure any individual devices that are going to be used have access to Google and CoSpaces Edu. You might need to check with your tech department.
- If you are renting out devices from the tech department or media center, make sure the machines have numbers, and students can save to those machines in a private cloud-based area where they can store their work and refer back to it for several music class periods.
- Share the goal and checklist with the students. You could either share it to students via Google Docs or pass out printed versions.
- Put all necessary material students will need to work on projects during class time on a table in the front of the room.

During Class

- When students arrive in class, begin a discussion about what the expectations will be for the next few lessons.
- Give students a refresher on how to use Google Slides to create their presentation.
- Show students how to use Audacity or GarageBand and how to record into it.
- Cue up your CoSpaces example and show it to the group. Explain that this will be part of their presentation. Show them how they will need to operate it to create their interactive experience.
  - o You can pass out the Google Cardboard to show students how your example looks in a 3D world.
- Have students choose the country they will be doing this project on or select it for them.

- Explain when the project is due and that there will be a celebration of presentations to signify the end of the project. (If you are collaborating with other teachers make sure to let students know they will see this project in different classes.)
- Share the goal and checklist with students and have them get out their devices and begin doing research.
- Give students time to apply the knowledge they have been learning in class to their work. Circulate around the room to guide and answer any questions they may have as they are working on the project.
- While students are working on their assignment, have them sign up for a presentation slot.
- Make sure students do not wait to record themselves singing or playing the song that they found. They will most likely run into a more significant line for the recording system the later that they wait for it.
- Encourage students to help each other to complete the project. Nothing is complete until presentation day. Even if they have practiced and said they are ready to go, they can always help a friend or practice again.
- On the day of presentations, do it up big! Decorate the room, play recorded music, get a couple of smartphones or iPod Touches for the Google Cardboard, or ask students to bring their phones in for this activity. If you want to go all out, get some snacks for students to enjoy while the presentations are going on. (Depending on how many students you have, you might have to take an extra class period of these presentations, or they can do this whole thing in groups so the presentations do not take as long.)
- Have the student or group come up and do their performance then demonstrate their VR universe using the interactive board. The presentation must consist of the student turning in their paper, presenting their slides (which include the video clip and recorded song), and showing their VR experience and explain what they did and explore it for the class.
- Afterward, they can put their experience on the phones or iPod Touches for other students in the class to look through.
- Invite administration and other teachers in to see students' hard work! Take lots of pictures and videos to share, too.
- If you have your devices for a more extended period, have the table with student's projects set out for a couple of days to share it with your school community. Encourage other teachers to stop by and view them!

Assessment Tips: In this activity, students will be producing a final product that demonstrates their knowledge of the country they were assigned. Assess that final product along with their presentation to the class. Pay close attention to the content of the presentation, along with how their 3D display works with their overall concept.

Audio Engineering

Recommended Grades: 7–12
Difficulty: Expert
Time: 2 to 3 class periods
Objective: Students will extend their knowledge of song composition into real-world application and discover more about careers in music during the process.

Resources

- Computer
- Interactive board
- Speakers
- Soundation.com or Soundtrap.com
- Individual devices
- Microphones (I recommend a couple of Blue Snowflake microphones)
- Headphones (you could ask students to bring their own)

When one thinks of music technology, they automatically think of what an audio engineer does on an almost-daily basis with software to edit their recordings. This activity is a great career connection, allowing students to immerse themselves into the world of music production and learn what it takes to create a song they hear on the radio or download to their phone. Learning how to record, mix, and produce tracks has become a big part of high school arts courses in music technology labs. Students can learn how to use a professional-style recording studio and create their works of art. I give my younger students a taste of a recording studio by cleaning out one of my closets to use as a recording booth, and setting up a microphone to an iPad. I set out a sign-up sheet and a pass from me to come during recess or before or after school, and they can come to record any songs they want (within reason) and then with their knowledge of how to edit audio from our projects in class, students can produce their tracks. They know they can always come to me for help.

Before Class

- Make sure you use this after a songwriting unit or with older students who have been in music class for a while. Students will need some background on the basics of music theory and how to piece it all together.
- Make sure your interactive board is up and working and has the proper software installed.
- If you do not have accounts to Soundation.com or Soundtrap.com, make sure to create accounts before you start this project.
- If you are not a 1:1 school make sure that you reserve either the computer lab or cart of devices beforehand (laptops are preferable).

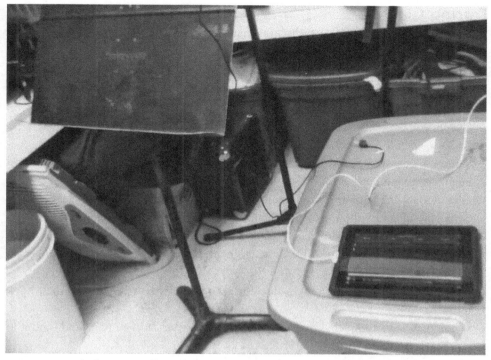

FIGURE 4.11 A look at my simple set up for my recording space (Photo Credit C. Dwinal)

- Ask students to bring in their headphones (make sure to have extras on hand for those who forget or do not have any to bring.)
- Get familiar with Soundation or Soundtrap and create examples to show the class.
- Create a quiet space with a microphone set up for students to record their hook in a quiet area.
- Create a goal for the project, and the checklist students need to complete to get there.
    - Goal: To record, mix, and produce a 2-minute piece of your music.
        - Write a short hook that you will use as the theme for this piece.
        - Make sure your piece has three to five layers, including your recorded hook.
        - You must have at least an A section and a B section.
        - Make sure your audio is pieced together correctly, and you use the editing tools to layer everything together.
        - Mix your piece into a final MP3.
        - Present the piece to class and describe your process.
- Before each class, make sure any individual devices that are going to be used have access to Soundation.com or Soundtrap.com.
- Make sure their work can be pulled up on the devices.
- Share the goal and checklist with the students.
- Remind students to get their headphones
- Take out all necessary material students will need to work on projects during class time.

During Class

- When students arrive in class, discuss what the expectations will be for the next few lessons.
- Give students a refresher on how to use Google Slides to create their presentation.
- Show students how to use Soundation.com and or Soundtrap.com and how to record and edit audio into it.
- Cue up your example on the board and show it to the group.
- Explain when the project is due and that they will present it to the class.
- Share the goal and checklist with students and have them get out their devices and begin creating their music.
- Give students time to apply the knowledge they have been learning in class to their work. Circulate the room to guide them and answer any questions they may have as they are working on the project.
- While students are working on their assignment, have them sign up for a time slot on the day of presentations.
- Make sure students do not procrastinate to record themselves performing their hook to use in their songs.
- When they have completed their work, they must export it as an MP3 and send it to you to put into a playlist.
- The day of presentations, have students come to the board to log in to their account, explain their work, and play their piece.
- When all presentations are complete, put them in a playlist to share with administrators and other teachers. You could also turn it into a CD to sell as a fundraising item for the arts program.

Assessment Tip: Ask students to present on the process they went through to create the MP3 and reflect on how it might be similar or different in a real-world situation. Assess students on the final MP3 they have designed and on their oral presentation on the reflection of the process.

5

Document Cameras

High-Low, Loud-Soft Shadow Movements

Recommended Grades: PreK–1
Difficulty: Beginner
Time: 15–20 min.
Objective: The class will show understanding of high and low and two-note compositions through whole-class movement and performing activities.

Resources
- Document camera
- Projector
- Paper
- Writing utensils
- Manipulatives
- Piano or other instruments that can play dynamics and tempo

Sometimes the best way to show a concept is to use a simple machine or tool like paper and building blocks. These things are big enough to be handled and used by any age safely. Tools like these are perfect for use with such a device as a document camera. You can show the movements from the activity below on a bigger screen for them to be able to see from any point in the room. You can compose using the manipulatives, and use the blocks as visual representations of the beats. There are many times that I use a document camera for things like going over quiz answers, or using the manipulatives to compose short beats. It is a simple universal tool that replaces the overhead projector and changed what used to be a squished time on the rug doing a demonstration with lots of little eyes looking over your shoulder, into

Interactive Visual Ideas for Musical Classroom Activities. Catherine Dwinal, Oxford University Press (2020). © Oxford University Press.
DOI: 10.1093/oso/9780190929855.001.0001

a proper presentation where everyone can see what you are doing and adequately understand the concept that you are trying to get across.

Before Class

- Make sure that the camera hooks up to the computer and can be seen clearly on the board. You might need to adjust the zoom on the picture if it's blurry.
- Make sure that you have a piece of paper on your document camera that has a grid drawn on it. Draw over the lines with a thicker black marker so it can be seen clearly by your students.
- Choose a manipulative that can be seen on the camera. You could use small blocks that you can get from the toy aisle in any store, or even Legos, or if you want to be silly, little plastic creatures that you can find through vendors like Oriental Trading. My students loved little plastic monsters, and I could use different ones to mean different musical symbols and so on.

During Class

- Draw a small grid on the piece of paper that is as many columns as you would like it to be but only two rows. Label one row High, and the other row Low, with a black marker.
  - Have student volunteers come up and place one block in each column and have them choose whether it goes in the High row or the Low row.
  - When they have completed the whole grid, have the class come up with a movement when they hear a high sound and an action when they hear a low tone (examples could be stand up/sit down, crouch low/jump high, etc.).
  - Have the volunteer point to each column to direct the class in their movements as you play the notes on the piano. Instruct students to get big when they hear the high notes and get small when they hear the low notes.
  - Repeat the same activity with different volunteers. Try to change it up and use other concepts like soft and loud and fast and slow.
- Draw a grid on your piece of paper that has as many columns as you would like but only two rows. Label the top one "Clap" and the bottom one "Pat."
  - Have student volunteers come up and place one block in each column where they can choose either pat or clap.
  - When the grid is filled in, perform the pattern pointing to each column as students either pat or clap to a beat.
- Draw a staff on your piece of paper that has as many measures as you would like but only one set of staff lines. Label the top one "Clap" and the bottom one "Pat."
  - Have student volunteers come up and place one monster in each beat in each measure.
  - When the staff is filled in, translate the notes that they put on the staff into something that students can play on Orff instruments!

Assessment Tip: Assess students on their comprehension of high and low and two-note compositions by their participation in the class activities and how they respond and move with their classmates.

Quick Instruction Visuals

Recommended Grades: PreK–5
Difficulty: Beginner
Time: 15–20 min.
Objective: The students will demonstrate knowledge of the topic being presented on the board by participating in the class discussion.

Resources

- Document camera
- Projector
- Paper or clear drawing paper
- Manipulatives
- Markers

I remember the days when I was in school (in the age of the dinosaurs when overhead projectors roamed the earth), when my teachers would write instructions and draw visuals on the plastic film and project it with the overhead projector for all the class to see, from drawing movement instructions to showing stage settings and even writing down step-by-step instructions for students to follow. You can find so many uses for something simple like this. There are times, especially when the Wi-Fi is a little glitchy, when I leave the Internet alone and use the document camera to show whatever visuals or instructions I need to give to students during the lessons. It is a great instructional tool when we do movement activities too, because I can draw visuals for concepts we are studying. Using a document camera is always an excellent plan B.

Before Class

- Make sure the document camera works and you can see it from the projector, and also make sure that you see the picture clearly on the board. You might need to adjust the zoom to see the whole scene and change the picture just in case it is fuzzy when projected.
- Use markers that are dark enough to be seen on the board.
- You can use a whiteboard surface or plastic film for this so you can wipe off the instructions and write new ones quickly if needed.

During Class

- Give directions on the board for students to see as soon as they walk into the class-room. If you are more paper-minded, you could also write your directions on paper to put it under the projector. Some examples of instructions:
  - Ask them to discuss a question with a neighbor.
  - Ask students to get a whiteboard and compose a rhythm on it and practice playing it.
  - Instruct students to find someone who likes the same style of music they do. Have them come up with a musical artist or song that defines that genre of music.
  - Have students get supplies out for a project or activity that you are going to do during the lesson.
  - Write out a seating chart of where you would like students to sit. Have them find their name and sit in their spot. This tool is useful for mixing things up with their seating to keep things interesting.
- Do you have an upcoming show? Have students come in and discuss stage settings. Draw where students will stand on the risers under the document camera and have them line up in real-time to practice.
  - Draw out the map of any specific movements on a piece of paper with markers (or use the manipulatives) to show students exactly where they need to move on stage during the show. This is especially helpful for transition or dance time.
  - Use the same strategy for the previously suggested activity to better explain to students square dancing formations during a square dancing unit! Draw the map of how the formations should move around the dance floor.

Assessment Tip: Assess students on their participation in the class discussion.

Hack Attack: Hacking Your Document Camera for Video Chatting and Pictures

Recommended Grades: PreK–12
Difficulty: Moderate
Time: 20 min.–2 hrs.
Objective: The class will use technology to share music and participate in discussions about what they are learning with others.

Resources

- Document camera
- Projector

- Skype
- Skype for the Classroom

When I first got one of the new document cameras my school received, I was excited about new tech but perplexed as to how to use it for my classroom. It wasn't until I found how to hack my camera and turn it into a webcam that I started to get more interested in it. At that time I had an older PC desktop that had no camera. When I finally had this tool set up, to turn it into a webcam I needed to switch the camera direction out and adjust the angle so instead of looking down at the table, it looked at the class or myself. From there, I did a lot of video chatting using Skype to talk with other teachers and students across the country and also used it as a camera for audio and video recording. There were a few times I used it for centers for students to record themselves straight to my computer, or I could also record myself on that camera if I knew in advance I was going to be absent, so the substitute teacher could play the video with my directions instead of having the sub verbally explain what I wanted them to do. This trick worked well until my computer was updated and had a video camera built in!

FIGURE 5.1 I easily converted my document camera into a web camera for video chatting (Photo Credit C. Dwinal)

Before Class

- Make sure the document camera works, and you can see it on the projector. Double-check that the picture is clear as well. You might need to adjust the zoom to see the whole picture and change the picture if it is fuzzy when projected.
- Check your systems to make sure you can reverse the camera and double-check that it operates with your video recording software and Skype.
- Make sure whatever you are showing on the screen can be seen in the video. If you are using smaller tools, you will need to bring them closer to the camera.
- If you are recording anything to show during class, make sure to record it beforehand for students to watch during the lesson.
- If you are using the document camera for a Skype performance, connect with another group or presenter who will video chat with your class. If you are in need of a place to find a teammate in this activity, go to https://education.microsoft.com/skype-in-the-classroom/overview to meet up with a like-minded educator to schedule a chat.

During Class

- Flip the camera toward the classroom. Find a place where it can face the class head-on rather than out to the side. You will be connecting with another class from another part of the world. Prep beforehand a piece of music that is a traditional folk song from your part of the globe. Give students a little background on it and teach them the song.
  o When students come in, have them sit down quietly in front of the camera so they can see the picture on the board.
  o Let students know that they will be talking with another class from a different part of the world. If your students are younger, let them know where their new friends live. If they are older, give students a chance to guess where the class/group is located.
  o Practice the folk song and review the facts about it before you connect with the class.
  o Remind the class that they are representing the school during this call, and they need to be on their best behavior.
  o Connect with the awaiting class and make introductions to one another.
  o The first class will give facts about their folk song and then sing it for the other group. The second class can ask questions about the song that the first-class sang and give positive comments.
  o Then the second class can do the same, giving the facts about their song and singing it for the first class. The first class will have the opportunity to ask questions as well.
  o Swap lyrics pages with the other teacher so the classes can learn each other's folk songs. Send a video of your class singing the other class's song to your teammate!

- For another activity, take the camera and flip it out, so it faces you.
  - Open up a video recording software. (If you are on a PC Filmora go is a good suggestion.)
  - Set up the document camera on your computer as a center. Have students record themselves answering an essential open-ended question. This activity helps them work on their critical thinking and communication skills. Some questions for them can be:
    - Why do we make music?
    - How has music made an impact on our culture?
    - Who is your favorite music artist? Why are they your favorite?
    - We have learned about a lot of composers; who has stood out to you?
    - Why do we always listen to music? Why does it make us feel the way we feel?
    - What do we need to create music?
    - What do our songs tell us about our history?
    - What must an object do to create a sound?
    - How does this melody make you feel?
    - Listen to the piece of music, what style is it? Why do you think it is that style of music?

Assessment Tip: Ask students to reflect on their sharing experience over video chat. Assess them on their participation in the activity as well as their reflection.

Manipulatives

Recommended Grades: K–3
Difficulty: Beginner
Time: 15–20 min.
Objective: Students will show proficiency in reading basic notation by reading and performing notation using graphic staff.

Resources
- Document camera
- Projector
- Staff paper
- Music note and rest manipulatives (could be pictures, bottle caps, Legos, foam dice, etc.)
- Glockenspiels

The document camera allows everyone to stay in their seats and be able to see everything clearly. I didn't find a use for it until I saw that it helped keep the peace when I was doing a demo for the class with smaller manipulatives or instruments. For example, I can put a

FIGURE 5.2 An example of some manipulatives I put under the document camera (Photo Credit C. Dwinal)

small glockenspiel under the camera to show students which bars to play. I keep it at a lower height for my younger students so they can access lessons like this.

Before Class

- Make sure that you have the proper document camera software downloaded.
- Hook up your document camera to the projector and make sure that it works. It should display on the projection any manipulatives you put under the camera. You might also need to adjust the zoom to see what is under the camera and focus the picture if it is a little fuzzy.
- Find staff paper that has bold and big enough staff lines to be seen through the projection from the board and that can fit your choice of manipulative. You most likely will have to draw your staff with a dark marker.
- If you do not have manipulatives made, go to Pinterest, find some that suit your lesson, and get crafting. The best kinds of manipulatives to show under a document camera will be mostly larger and darker laminated pictures of notes and rests, or smaller manipulatives like foam dice that have the notes and rests drawn with a bolder marker. You could also hit up the dollar store to find smaller toys that will work under the camera.

During Class

- Have the students sit in rows in front of the board so everyone can see what is projected and be able to reach the document camera. I recommend putting the document camera on a sturdy table that is student height.
- With this activity, they will be composing and using their instruments to play their class creations. Have the instruments nearby, but compose first. Pass out the instruments when it is time to play.
- Start with you as the teacher doing the first one or two compositions to show students what to do. Compose a short melody or rhythm using the manipulatives by putting them on the staff that you have drawn. Have students discover how the piece is supposed to be played together before playing it as a class. Do body percussion first before you pass out instruments.
- Once you and the class have played together a few times with compositions that you have created, it is time to give the students a chance. Start taking volunteers to compose using the manipulatives and have the class discover how it will sound before they play it together. Pass out instruments and play what they wrote together as an ensemble. Be sure to reflect on each composition. An excellent reflection strategy is to have someone give one positive comment about the piece as a quick confidence booster.
- If you want to go a step further, give student volunteers complete control over the activity. Have them compose their piece, teach it to the class, and then lead the class as they play it together as an ensemble. It also is a way to help students hone their leadership skills and how to communicate to a class as they figure out how to convey what they want their audience to do with their piece.

Assessment Tip: Ask student volunteers to lead the class. Use this as a time to make your way around the room to sit with small groups and assess students as they participate in the activity. Use a mobile device and spend a minute recording each student on video. Go back later and review the footage to assess their proficiency in reading basic notation.

Note Identify Flashcard Game

Recommended Grades: K–3
Difficulty: Beginner
Time: 15–20 min.
Objective: Students will demonstrate knowledge of notes and rests by identifying visuals on the board at a rapid-fire pace.

Resources

- Document camera
- Projector
- Music note and rest flashcards

With larger groups, sometimes not everyone can see the great manipulatives you want to show them. This is where technology can come into play. A document camera helps project the image so students can see more clearly and in a calmer manner, without having to jump over one another to see what is going on

Before Class

- Check your document camera to make sure that the connections are good and you can see the picture clearly on the board. You might need to adjust the zoom to see the whole scene and focus the picture just in case it is fuzzy.
- Double-check the projector placement. If you have a larger ensemble, you will need to make sure it is projected on a larger surface for the back of the room to see.
- Make sure the flashcards you are going to use are dark enough and big enough for the whole class to view at once.

During Class

- Tell your students this is practice time for learning to quickly naming their notes and rests. (You can also use this as a great exit ticket–type activity to see where the class is in recognizing their notes and rests.)
- Start by putting one card on the document camera at a time and have student volunteers answer what musical symbol is on the card.
- Make a half circle if you have the space; if not, you can do this in rows. Ask a student to identify the note or rest on the card. If they get it right, they get to start the game. If they get it wrong, then keep going around until one student gets it correct.
- The first student who gets the correct answer stands behind or next to the next student. Put a flashcard under the camera, and the first one to answer correctly gets to move on. If the student who got the last question correct gets the next one wrong, they have to sit in that student's chair or stand in their spot and the student who got it correct moves forward. This activity is pretty much a simple game of "Around the World."

Assessment Tip: Before students leave class, ask each student to answer three rapid-fire flashcards before they are allowed to line up to leave. Assess them on their number of correct answers and speed of answering.

Puppet Show

Recommended Grades: 1–3
Difficulty: Beginner
Time: 30–40 min.
Objective: Students will demonstrate a more in-depth knowledge of *Peter and the Wolf* by creating their version of the story to perform like a puppet show for the class.

Resources

- Document camera
- Projector
- Finger puppets
- Simple storyboard worksheet
- Pencils
- *Peter and the Wolf* audio track

We, as humans, are inherently drawn to a good story. Stories in the music room help students identify with classical and modern-day pieces. They see words and pictures in their head as the music plays. We think of puppet shows from the times of the Middle Ages and Renaissance periods, that were performed on the streets: live storytelling that brought stories to life. Today's kids still love them.

Before Class

- Hook up your document camera to the projector and make sure that it works. It should display any manipulatives you put under the camera.
- Take a simple storyboard worksheet and make a copy for each student. Also, make sure to have pencils and coloring materials for the storyboards.
- Have students learn the story of *Peter and the Wolf* and listen to the piece before this activity.
- Make sure to gather pictures of *Peter and the Wolf* characters or get your art teacher to help you! Put all the characters on to one or two worksheets for students to color and cut them out. Cut out one set for yourself and have your 2D versions of puppets ready for this activity! Have multiple sets available for students to use if you will not have time in class to create puppets, or if you are doing this activity with a younger crowd.
- You might also find *Peter and the Wolf*–style finger puppets for this activity that can be available for students to use as well.

During Class

- Have the piece playing as students are entering the classroom and getting to their seats.
- The goal of the activity is to create a short puppet show showing their interpretation of the story of *Peter and the Wolf*. Take out a few of the finger puppets and do a short puppet show to show students an example of what they will be doing.
- Have them either do this project individually or in small groups.
- Give each a storyboard worksheet and drawing materials and ask them to fill the storyboard with their summary of the tale of *Peter and the Wolf*.
- Student goals of the activity:
  - Create a six-panel storyboard about *Peter and the Wolf*
  - Color and cut out your 2D puppets.
  - Prepare a short puppet show to show the class.

- When every student has finished or has had a sufficient amount of time, call the students back to prepare for the puppet show shenanigans. If you wanted to go above and beyond, shut out the lights, put fancy curtains up next to the projector—even pop some popcorn.
- Students will need the paper puppets they created during work time for this. Or students could instead choose the finger puppets they want out of the pile and then perform their short puppet show under the document camera.
- One at a time, have the students come up. To add ambiance, play a recording of Prokofiev's *Peter and Wolf* when students are transitioning from one person to the next. Students will be able to see the puppet show on the projector screen while the student is presenting on the document camera.

Assessment Tip: Assess students on their understanding of *Peter and the Wolf* by Prokofiev and their understanding of themes and variations by their new take on the story of *Peter and the Wolf*.

Notating a Piece of Music

Recommended Grades: 5–12
Difficulty: Beginner
Time: 5–20 min.
Objective: Students will show understanding in ensemble rehearsal techniques and score study by participating in ensemble rehearsal and discussions.

Resources
- Document camera
- Projector
- Paper
- Dark writing utensil (pencil with a darker lead)

The document camera allows you to put your physical printed scores of music under the camera and point out the specific place you want to work on in rehearsal. It takes the guessing out of where you want them to start when you can show them physically.

Before Class
- Check your document camera to make sure that the connections are good and you can see the picture clearly on the board. You might need to adjust the zoom to see the whole scene and change the picture if it is fuzzy when projected.
- Double-check the projector placement. If you have a larger ensemble, you will need to make sure it is projected on a larger surface for the back of the room to see.

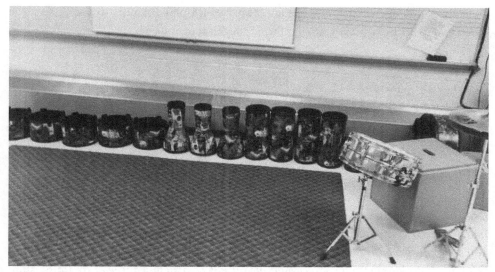

FIGURE 5.3 Instruments lined up ready to be played (Photo Credit C. Dwinal)

- Make sure the drawing utensils you are using to make notations are dark enough for students to see from anywhere in the room. Usually, if you press down firmly enough on a pencil, students can see the notations better.

During Class
- Conduct the rehearsal as usual. Have the document camera on and possibly have a copy of each of the instrument section's parts.
  - When you want to rehearse a part of the piece that does not have a measure number, stop the ensemble and put your score under the document camera. Point out precisely where you want the group to start.
  - When a specific part comes up that you would like to alter or work on, put your score under the document camera and mark up where you would like students to make marks with their pencil.

Assessment Tip: Assess students on their participation in rehearsal and the ability to make changes based on the visuals presented to them during practice time.

Drawing Storyboards

Recommended Grades: 6–8
Difficulty: Moderate
Time: 20–45 min.

Objective: Students will demonstrate aural musicianship by listening to a selected piece of music and creating a story based on what they hear.

Resources

- Document camera
- Projector
- Paper
- Markers
- Classical piece of music

Why not use music as the starting point and let creativity and imagination run free? Drawing a storyboard could lead to a more significant and more in-depth project. Imagine making a movie with this storyboard, or doing a puppet show, or even a play. You can show students how to move forward from an idea to a full product, using critical thinking and planning skills. You could also use it as a significant lead to a discussion about different careers that they could aspire to. You can show them skills that will travel with them for a lifetime. Take the time to let them lead, and if they fail, it is a learning experience!

FIGURE 5.4 I have a box of whiteboards ready for students at all times (Photo Credit C. Dwinal)

Before Class

- Give students some prior knowledge of a famous piece of music like *Carnival of the Animals, The Nutcracker*, or "In the Hall of the Mountain King," a piece that has a story idea.
  - You might need to download the piece of music you are going to choose through a music service like iTunes or Google Play store, especially if your Wi-Fi is not the best. If your Wi-Fi works well, you could also find it on a streaming service like Spotify.
- Make sure you have markers that will draw dark, to show up the best while using the document camera.
- Gather all the necessary art materials.
- Create a storyboard grid template similar to Figure 5.5 to send out to students on their devices. (Unless you are using pencil and paper, then create a worksheet for this activity.)
- Rent the individual devices you need. For this activity, you will only need a few (one for each group) unless you would like to vary the activity and have one for each student. Alternately, you could provide just pencil and paper for everyone.

Storyboard Worksheet

Name:
Classroom Teacher:
Music:
Title of Story:

1	2	3	4
5	6	7	8

FIGURE 5.5 Worksheet Example to use for activity

- Check your document camera to make sure that the connections are good and you can see the picture clearly on the board. You might need to adjust the zoom to see the whole scene and focus the picture if it is fuzzy when projected.

During Class

- Have students listen to the piece of music and imagine what story it is trying to tell them. Ask students the question, "What do you imagine is happening while this piece of music is playing? What story is it trying to tell you?"
  - o Put a piece of paper on the document camera and take suggestions from the class as to what you should draw in your scene. Have each volunteer tell you only one thing to add. Stand back after you have taken a few suggestions, and ask students if the scene fits the music. If not, why? Also, what story could this scene tell?
    - Variation: Draw a few boxes and take suggestions from the students as to what is happening in the story. Allow them to be as imaginative as possible, to see what adventure they can create as a class.
  - o Allow students to try it on their own. Pass out devices with the storyboard template on them (or paper and pencils) and play the piece of music again.
  - o Let students take a few minutes to sketch out their stories. Let them color them and write text in the boxes.
  - o If some have finished early, have them partner up and chat with each other about their adventures.
  - o Bring the class together to talk about what they really think is going on in the music. Have volunteers show their sketches. Ask students to turn in their stories.

Extended Activity

- o Piece together everyone's views about what is happening in the piece of music into a whole class basic outline.
- o Have students break into groups and flesh out the overall story using the outline you used as a class. Have each group use the Book Creator app to put together their story into a book. Have each group come up and share their story when completed.
  - o Another variation of this is to create a short story yourself that will fit within your storyboard template. Write a short story that has some gaps that can be filled in on it and has room for music in the background.
- o When students are coming into class, have your story up on the document camera.
- o Ask them to read it and to start thinking about what needs to be added to it. Have the group discuss with a neighbor what needs to be added.

o Have them get out individual devices, share the story with them, and ask students to type up the story, adding in the details they feel would best fit.

o Share the storyboard worksheet with them and have students put the story they wrote out into a visual format. Give them a sufficient amount of time to do this but encourage them to be clear and concise.

o Have them print out their final storyboards.

o Once they have completed their storyboards, have students play several pieces of well-known classical music (you can create a list for them to choose from.)

o Have students choose one piece that best reflects the story that they wrote from the prompt.

o Have volunteers come up one at a time and put their printed storyboards under the document camera and explain what their story is about while playing the corresponding piece of music.

o If you would like to put stories up on display, put all of the printed storyboards on your bulletin board. Put a QR code up next to each storyboard that links to a YouTube version of the music and encourages those who are looking at the board to scan the code and play the music.

Assessment Tip: Using the storyboards that students create, assess their understanding of the piece they were listening to by how well their story corresponds with the music.

Ensemble Practice Instruction

Recommended Grades: 6–12
Difficulty: Beginner
Time: 15–20 min.
Objective: The class will demonstrate proficiency in time management of rehearsals and sight-reading by following visuals on the board.

Resources
• Document camera
• Projector
• Paper
• Dark marker or writing utensil

This activity is primarily for educators who may have a poorly placed whiteboard in their room, which students have difficulty seeing. Being able to project to a bigger surface can help students see the directions better, and is even more helpful in an ensemble setting when you might have a hundred students packed into one room. You can project instructions, warm-ups, and order of pieces on the wall for all to see.

Before the Rehearsal

- Check your document camera to make sure that the connections are good and you can see the picture clearly on the board. You might need to adjust the zoom to see the whole scene and focus the picture if it is fuzzy when projected.
- Double-check the projector placement. If you have a larger ensemble, you will need to make sure it is projected on a larger surface for the kids at the back of the room to see.
- Make sure the markers you are using to write directions or make notations are dark enough for students to see from anywhere in the room.
- Figure out what music you will be using and what warm-ups the group will be doing for the rehearsal.

During the Rehearsal

- Use the projection system to write down what you want the ensemble to practice for the rehearsal. Make notes of specific parts that you want to focus on and any reminders for the students. An example of this might be:

Good morning!

Today we will be prepping for the upcoming concert in two weeks so please have all your music ready to go. Also, remember to take a concert reminder home with you today. They are on the table next to the door on your way out.

Warm-ups today

- *Standard of Excellence Page 2, Exercises 7, 8, and 9*

Concert order as follows:

- *Bohemian Rhapsody*
- *Star Wars Medley*
- *Jurassic World*
- *Singing in the Rain*
- *At the Movies Medley*
- *The Greatest Show*

Make sure that you have all the music pulled up before I take the podium. Remember to ask me any concert questions after rehearsal!

- Use a plain piece of paper and draw out a short rhythm and sight-reading exercise that you want to practice with your ensemble.

- Have students get their instruments out and get ready to warm up. Have them warm up on scales until you are prepared to start.

Assessment Tip: If you are looking for an assessment opportunity for this activity, perform an observational assessment on their sight-reading skills. Write out a sight-reading melody or rhythm under the camera and have each section play or say it one at a time. Observe each student on how well they read the music.

6

Streaming Media Players

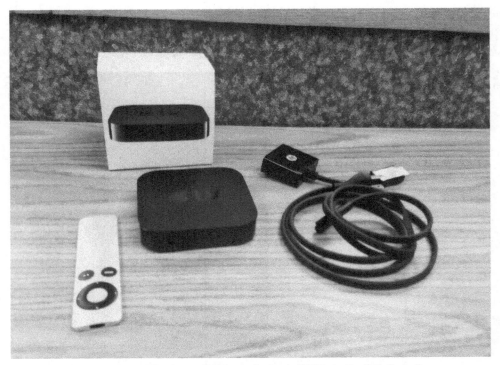

FIGURE 6.1 My streaming media player of choice is the Apple TV (Photo Credit C. Dwinal)

Remote Desktop Activities

Recommended Grades: PreK–12
Difficulty: Moderate
Time: 5 min.–Full class

Interactive Visual Ideas for Musical Classroom Activities. Catherine Dwinal, Oxford University Press (2020). © Oxford University Press.
DOI: 10.1093/oso/9780190929855.001.0001

Objective: Students will demonstrate knowledge of the concepts by completing activities presented on mobile devices.

Resources

- iPads or Android tablets
- Projector
- Computer with the desktop streamer on it
- Doceri or Splashtop apps

Doceri, a remote desktop control app, is one of the best tools that I use in my room. I did not have access to an interactive board for a long time. I had a projector and a computer that was at least eight years old. When I finally discovered what these remote desktop apps could do, it completely changed the way I conducted class; I was able to break away from the front of the room and move around. I was able to turn my iPad into a remote control for the projector screen. I could take it around the room and have students interact with what was on the board from their seats. I could show students different slides or start and stop music on the board from anywhere in the room. I could sit with fourth graders who were having trouble with their recorders and still control the song on the board for the rest of the class. It was even better when I sat with my kindergartners in a circle and could still control

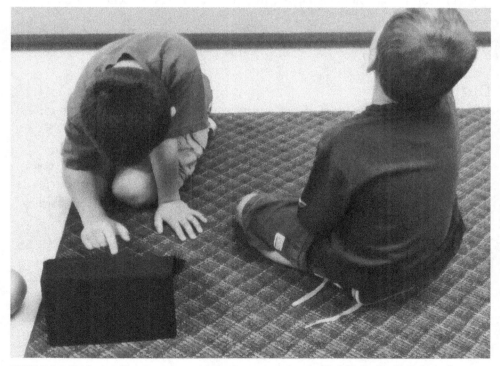

FIGURE 6.2 Students taking turns on an interactive game using the iPad (Photo Credit C. Dwinal)

the music or pictures on the board. It cut the cords that kept me in front of the room and allowed me to be more involved in my instruction! There are other apps out there, such as Splashtop (another type of remote desktop app) that I use heavily in my teaching. Splashtop has several options that make it an excellent tool for the classroom. It is a tool that I use almost daily; since I don't have an interactive board, I had to get creative to do interactive technology-based activities. iPads are more readily available for schools; they are more mobile and cheaper to purchase in bulk.

Before Class

- You will not need to use your streaming media player for this! The mobile device connects directly to your computer.
- Make sure to download the desktop app to your computer and download the app to your mobile device before trying this with a class—the desktop app talks to the app on your mobile device to allow the two to connect over a Wi-Fi connection. Doceri, in particular, has the option to mark up a screen and create lessons and other visuals that you can mirror from the device to your computer. Doceri is a little on the cheaper side while Splashtop, although a little more expensive, is more robust.
- Make sure your mobile device can connect to your computer over a Wi-Fi connection. When you get it working, you can connect to your computer from far away. If you have any trouble, contact your tech department for help. Many times I set up my lessons for the day on my computer from halfway across the school in the middle of duty.
- Before class, connect your device to your computer and make sure you can manipulate what is on the screen.

During Class

- Use an interactive resource such as QuaverMusic.com. They have an extensive library of interactive lyrics activities. Choose one of their recorder activities for students to try.
  - Bring up the fingering chart in the program and using Doceri, click on the notes the students will be using in the song while you sit with some students who need some extra guidance. Have students practice the fingerings first and then start by playing each one of the notes that they will be using in the song.
  - Next, use the Recorder Olympics to play the accompaniment track and have students play simple rhythms to get prepared to play the piece.
  - Click the interactive lyrics page. Press Play from where you are in the room and have the class play the song, following along as the notes are highlighted for them as you help others play together and get the attention that they need. (There are many times I am able to walk to the far corner of the room—to the students who are farthest away from me—and interact and play with them!)

- Take Noteflight and set up a new score.
  - Use this activity to learn about students' understanding of music theory and how they practically apply it.
  - Connect your device to the computer using Doceri and ask students to think about a one-measure melody they would compose.
  - Take volunteers one at a time to compose one measure on the device. You can hand them the device at their seat to keep the class under control. You could even pass the device around the circle to do a rapid-fire composition activity.
  - Have students reflect on the composition by listening to it and having a discussion about how it sounds.
- Set up your lessons for the day.
  - Make sure the Splashtop app is open on your device as well as your desktop. You should know when you open up the app on your device and see your desktop on your screen.
  - Manipulate the desktop from your app in any part of the school, while doing morning or lunch duties.
- Play games from your device.
  - Bring up an interactive game on the board and connect your mobile device using Splashtop. There are many different resources you can use for this activity. See the Resources section for suggestions.
    - Bring up the activity and have the whole class participate in it. You can have students sit in their regular seats and pass the device around for everyone to have a turn interacting with the board.
    - Use it as a center! Have the activity on the projector and connect it to your device. Have the small groups manipulate the activity from the device while on the floor. They can have one person on the device at a time as the rest watch from the projector.
- Creating lessons in Doceri
  - You can create experiences before class while inside of Doceri to share with students by mirroring to your device using the app to the streamer on your desktop.
  - The lessons you can create inside of the Doceri app are more of a Draw My Life animation style. Create an experience in the app to show students or draw the mini-lesson as you have students in front of you. Some examples of mini Doceri lessons you could do:
    - An overview of a single note or rest. Go over what it looks like, how many beats it has, how it fits into a measure, etc.
    - Have a lesson on how to compose a measure in 4/4, 3/4, or 2/4 time.
    - Help students discover five fun facts about a composer or musical genre.

- Discuss what distinguishes a particular historical period.
- Provide some cultural background on a song they are performing or singing.
- Build quick overview lessons about certain musical symbols and other important musical aspects.

Assessment Tip: With the activity you are doing in class, make sure to give each student a chance to do the exercise. Assess them on their participation.

Interactive Instruments

Recommended Grades: PreK–12
Difficulty: Beginner
Time: 5–20 min.
Objective: Students will show proficiency in music performance and instrument knowledge by playing their digital instruments in an ensemble setting.

Resources
- Streaming media player
- One iPad or Android tablet
- Projector
- Virtuoso Piano, Guitar Elite, Easy Xylophone, Hand Drums apps

I love using interactive instruments for mobile devices, mixing traditional music-making practices and digital tools to engage technology-driven learners. You can also accommodate many students with physical disabilities by having them play instruments on a mobile device in their lap as opposed to trying to play the real instrument. Many students who have special needs carry around a communication device such as a tablet. You can ask their teacher to get one or two instrument apps on that device for those students to play during class. Not only does it add another level of color to the ensemble, but it allows you to differentiate instruction and be able to include the student in all activities. Interactive instruments, especially on a mobile device, will enable teachers to modify learning and create more variations in their instructional techniques. There are hundreds of interactive instrument apps available, so there are a lot of choices that you can give your students.

Before Class
- Connect your streaming media player to your projector and make sure it works properly.
- Make sure your mobile devices can connect to your streaming media player. (If you would like sound through the system and not just playing from the device, you will need to plug it directly into your speakers or use Bluetooth.)

FIGURE 6.3 You could take it a step further like me and create your own instrument from recycled materials and connect it to your interactive instrument (Photo Credit C. Dwinal)

- Download the suggested apps in the materials list or if you have other preferred apps, download those (or make sure your IT department has fulfilled your request for the app downloads.)
- Test the sound on the instrument through the system. You may need to adjust levels to be palatable to your student's ears or to blend in with the rest of the students in the group.
- Before the class, make sure that your mobile devices have the apps downloaded and are operating correctly.
- Connect one of the devices and make sure it operates on your streaming media player.
- Connect the sound to your speaker system and test it one more time.

During Class
- Use the xylophone or piano apps to demonstrate playing techniques such as how to hold the mallets or how. to place fingers on the instrument.
    - Have students at the Orff instruments or pianos.
    - Bring up the corresponding app and connect your device to your projector.
    - Use the app as a tool to show students techniques or melodies to play together. You can also use it to play along with the class.

- Some tricks if you are a "traveling" teacher who goes from room to room:
  - Bring an adapter with you to connect with the projection system in the room. (Or if the teacher has a streaming media player you can connect to that!)
  - Hook the device up to the projection system and plug it into the sound system.
  - Use the device as your instrument to play along with students or accompany basic vocal warm-ups (certainly not a perfect substitute for a piano or full Orff instrument but more comfortable to carry around and perfect to play simple chords!)
- Using interactive instruments as a handy tool:
  - You can have your instrument handy during an ensemble rehearsal. Use it as a tuning instrument if you are rehearsing with an instrumental ensemble or use it as a pitch pipe for vocal groups.
  - Use it as a teaching tool when talking about notes on a staff. This tool is best while teaching students about melody. Show them how the notes move around on the staff.
  - If you have a student with different needs, who is limited while playing a physical instrument, have them use one of the instrument apps so they can play with the rest of the class.

Assessment Tip: Assess students on their performance using the digital instrument, paying close attention to how they adapt to the different interface and play with others in the ensemble.

Explain Everything

Recommended Grades: K–6
Difficulty: Moderate
Time: 15–20 min.
Objective: Students will demonstrate learned knowledge through the creation of a final video product.

Resources
- Streaming media player
- iPads or Android tablets
- Projector
- Explain Everything app (Found on the App Store or Google Play Store)

I was introduced to this app several years ago by a dear friend and mentor who used it as a great assessment tool for her younger students. They were able to draw, for example, a simple rhythm in 4/4 ,meter, while saying the rhythm out loud as it was being recorded. This app, as well as many other apps, creates an actual physical product that shows off student knowledge. Think of it as a way for students to teach you a way to practice sharing their knowledge with others.

Before Class

- Connect your streaming media player to your projector and make sure it works properly. (If you would like sound, you will need to plug your mobile device directly into your speakers.)
- Make sure your mobile devices can connect to your streaming media player.
- Download the Explain Everything app to your devices (or make sure your IT department has fulfilled your request for the app download).
- Create an example of the project to show students what the expectation is for the lesson activity.
- For better audio, acquire a few microphones that can connect to your devices.
- Right before the class, make sure your mobile devices have the Explain Everything app on them and they are operating correctly.
- Connect one of the devices and make sure it operates on your streaming media player. (You will need to plug the device into the speaker system of your projector to hear the recordings.)

During Class

- Students will need prior knowledge of reading and writing rhythms for this activity.
  - Have the app open on a device and ready to go for class.
  - Before going into the app, use either some old favorite melody flashcards or write different rhythms on the board. Have students say and use body percussion together. If you want to go a little further with the activity, have student volunteers come up to speak and play for the class.
  - Project the app on the screen and demonstrate for students how to draw and record in the app. Give them the task of composing one measure in 4/4 meter and then play or say the rhythm.
  - An alternative could be for students to listen to a melody you play on the piano and draw the melodic contour on the app, then sing what they drew on a neutral syllable.
    - Have student volunteers share their work by posting it on the board to share with the class.
- Do a composer version of "Draw My Life." (This would be best with three to six students.)
  - Made famous by many YouTubers in 2017, "Draw My Life" is when a person makes a sketch stop-motion video about their lives. It may describe their life from the beginning or just fun facts about themselves. Start by making an example

yourself to show the students. It can be about yourself or a composer of your choice.

- o Bring students together when they arrive to class and show them your example of a "Draw My Life" video. Explain to students how you did it and what your process was.
- o Assign each student a composer or give them a list to choose.
- o Give each student a device or have them bring their own if you are a 1:1 school with tablets. (Make sure the devices have the Explain Everything app on them. If they do not, you will need to put in a request to your IT department to load the app on the devices before this activity.)
- o Go through a quick demonstration of how to operate the app and the different activities that they can do with it.
- o Let them know that they will be doing their "Draw My Life" with the composer they chose. Goals that they will need to meet:
  - Research their composer and come up with three to five facts about his or her life.
  - Come up with their plan to draw their composer's life video. They will need to know their plan before recording.
- o Have students find a quiet corner and start recording. Remind them that it doesn't have to be perfect, just creative and informative!
- o Give students quiet spaces around the room to record their videos as you walk around guiding those who need assistance.
- o Afterward, have students mirror their device to the projector one by one to play their videos for their classmates.
- o Have them share their videos with you so you can compile the videos later to share with your school community.
- Have students walk through how instruments make a sound.
  - o This activity can be a great science of sound project or STEAM connection. Do this activity after a discussion about the instruments of the orchestra or a unit on the instrument families. Students will need some background on what each instrument is and how it works.
  - o Have students pick an instrument of the orchestra that they will do their video about.
  - o Give each student a device or have them bring their own if you are a 1:1 school with tablets. (Make sure they have the Explain Everything app on them. If not, you will need to put in a request to your IT department.)
  - o Goals for this activity are:
    - To research how their instrument creates sound.
    - To use the Explain Everything app to explain how the instrument makes a sound while they draw a diagram of how the sound travels through it.
  - o Have students find a quiet corner and start recording. Remind them that it doesn't have to be perfect, just creative and informative!

- Give students quiet spaces around the room to record their videos as you walk around, guiding those who need assistance.
- Afterward, have students mirror their device to the projector one by one to play their videos for their classmates.
- Have them share their videos with you so you can compile their projects later to share with your school community.

- Have students pick a classical piece of music and draw the story they hear.
  - Use devices as an alternative to pencil and paper, and ask them to listen to a piece of music and reflect on what they hear by drawing the story they think the music is trying to convey.
  - Mirror your device to the board, and play a piece of music. Start drawing a scene on the app as the music plays. Comment here and there about the music and what you are drawing, as students watch.
  - Give students each a device or have them bring their own if you are a 1:1 school with tablets. (Make sure they have the Explain Everything app on them. If not, you will need to put in a request to your IT department.)
  - Together, play the music again and while you do the same thing, have students do their version along with you.
  - Share some volunteer story videos on the board by mirroring them, and discuss them.
  - Goals for this activity are:
    - To listen to the chosen piece of music.
    - To use the Explain Everything app to respond to the piece of music while drawing the story; to explain what they think the music is trying to tell its audience.
  - Have students find a quiet corner and start recording. Remind them that it doesn't have to be perfect, just creative and informative! Walk around the room and guide those who need extra assistance.
  - Afterward, have students mirror their device to the projector one by one to play their videos for their classmates.
  - Have them share their videos with you so you can compile the videos later to share with your school community.

Assessment Tip: In this activity, they are creating a tangible final product that will share the knowledge they have learned. Have them share their videos with you and assess their competency of the subject based on the content of their final product.

Metaverse Assessments and Word Hunt

Recommended Grades: K–8
Difficulty: Expert
Time: 15–20 min.

Objective: Students will demonstrate competency of a specific subject through augmented reality (AR) activities by either participating in them or creating them.

Resources

- Streaming media player
- iPads or Android tablet
- Projector
- Metaverse app

Virtual Reality and Augmented Reality have started to go mainstream and have been sought after for innovative use in classes. I remember playing with what was then called Aurasma for hours just for fun, before figuring out what to use it for in class. When I did start using it, the look on students' faces when they hovered their devices over the targets was one of absolute wonder. Students could take a device up to the board, open the app, and then point the camera at the word and a video would pop up explaining the definition of it. Students could use the board often when they forgot what the keyword was and needed a reminder. They can do this in the middle of class, especially when I am occupied with another activity. Now you see AR and VR becoming even more mainstream with big companies such as Apple and Adobe building tools to make classroom use even easier. You can turn what was once a 2D lesson into a 4D learning experience.

Before Class

- Connect up your streaming media player to your projector and make sure it works properly together. (If you would like sound, you will need to plug the device directly into your speakers)
- Make sure your mobile devices can connect to your streaming media player.
- Download the Metaverse app to your device and to the student devices (or make sure your IT department has fulfilled your request for the app download).
- Create or take a quiz that you plan on giving to your students. Take the answers from that quiz you've created and put them in a list in a separate note.
- For every correct answer on your list, make sure there is a wrong answer to go along with it.
- Log into the Metaverse Studio and create targets for each of the right and wrong answers you have listed. All wrong answers have one target, and all right answers have a different one. Print out each of these answers on paper.
- If you feel that you need some backup because you feel slightly uncomfortable doing this activity by yourself right now, ask someone from your technology department to help you get set up for this activity and then assist you.
- If you are going to do the word hunt, experience the app yourself, and create a few examples of a word hunt before you create one for the students. You can also check out premade puzzles and quests that were made by other educators like yourself.

- Some examples of word hunts and challenges that you could do:
  - Create a search that tests student's knowledge of notes and rests. Have them follow the quiz around the room as they answer questions about the topic.
  - Guess the instrument or composer! Ask questions that describe a specific instrument or composer. Have students write their final answer on the board after they finish the search of who or what they think it is.
  - Have students search for keywords that you have been teaching them throughout a unit or a semester. Ask them the definitions to the words or flip it around and give them the descriptions and ask for the word.
  - You could also create a word hunt that helps students answer an essential question. You can ask smaller, more detailed questions that lead up to the more significant questions.
- Right before students come in, separate the wrong and right answers into two separate piles.
- Make sure that your mobile devices have the Metaverse app on them, and that they are operating correctly.
- Connect one of the devices and make sure it operates on your streaming media player.
- If you need to rent devices from your media center, make sure to get them before class. If you are a 1:1 school, make sure that the students are reminded to bring their devices to class.
- If you are doing the word hunt, make sure to check the app for your word hunt and make sure that it is operational on the device.
- If you need some tech assistance, ask your technology coach or technology department representative to come to class to help.

During Class

- You can use this as an informal assessment or a check for understanding.
  - Divide the class into two teams. Let them know that this is a quiz game show and they will be competing against each other.
  - Bring up the first question and ask team number one, then give them the two options for the answer.
  - Have the team choose a representative from their group to come up and point the device camera at one of the answers. They will know if it is right or wrong depending on what target comes up on the device. If they get it right, they get the point, and if the group gets it wrong, they do not.
  - Then the next team goes and does the same process.
  - Team with the most correct at the end wins!
    - Make sure students get equal turns to try the devices.
    - Make sure you have the device connected to the screen so all students can experience the answers and graphics that come up!
- To start the word hunt with your students:
  - Mirror your device to the board to show students what the app is. Give them a tutorial on how it works. There are many video tutorials on YouTube

- o Give them the goal of this activity: to follow the prompts in the app and answer questions that pop up.
- o Pass out or have students get devices themselves. Ask them to open the Metaverse app and instruct them on how to get to the hunt that you created.
- o Let them start and explore. Make sure to move around the room to facilitate and guide the students as they walk around answering the questions. If a student finishes early, have them either help another student or give them another hunt to do. There are fun ones made by others on the app that the students can try.
- o Bring all students back together and bring the hunt on the board by mirroring your device and going through it together as a class so students can see the right answers.
- Have students build their own word hunt!
  - o Have students come into class and sit in their regular spots as they wait for instruction.
  - o Mirror your device to the board to show students what the app is. Give them a tutorial on how it works. There are many video tutorials on YouTube about how to operate the app and the studio side of it that you can share with students.
  - o Give them the goal of this activity: To create a word hunt based on a specific topic that one of their classmates can play.
  - o Pass out or have students get devices themselves. Ask them to open the studio and instruct them on how to get started. Give students a limit on how many questions they can create to manage time. Walk around the room to guide and facilitate the activity.
  - o When students have finished, have them share their hunts.
  - o Ask student volunteers to mirror their word hunt to the board to share and then let classmates navigate to the quests they would like to experience on their own devices. Give students time to explore and experiment with a few different ones.
  - o Bring everyone back together to reflect and try a few of the word hunts on the board.
  - o Send some of the hunts to administrators and other faculty members to have them try it out!

Assessment Tips: Create or find a word hunt for students to complete. Have students complete the hunt and then have them self-assess by going over the answers as a class. Or use this as a comprehension check. Or have students create their word hunt and assess them on the content and flow of their final product.

Recording and Showing Performances and Informances

Recommended Grades: K–12
Difficulty: Beginner
Time: Concert time

Objective: Students will show proficiency in reflecting on performances by participating in class discussions using recorded visuals.

Resources
- Streaming media player
- iPads or Android tablet
- Projector

The easiest thing that you can do with a mobile device is to open a camera app, set it up for performance then hit Record to capture the special moments. After capturing the action, watch the performance video right on the device, then upload it to a file library or send it to your secretary for PR or sharing purposes. I still have performance videos on my desktop from my teaching days, which I watch when I miss the classroom. Once I prepared a flash mob for my elementary kids to do during an all-school assembly. Our school mascot was the tiger, so we used an arrangement of Katy Perry's "Roar." We surprised all the teachers and parents who were there. Our PE teacher filmed the whole thing and I was able to edit it right on my iPad and post it to our school Google Drive account for the teachers to see!

Performance Reflection Worksheet

Name:
Date:
Class:

Watch the playback of your performance and answer the following questions.

- What are three things you see that you are doing great?

- What are two things that you are doing that you could improve and how will you improve them?

- Compliment one other person on the point out something they are doing very well.

FIGURE 6.4 Getting ready to record a performance!

Before Class
- Connect your streaming media player to your projector and make sure it works properly. (If you would like sound, you will need to plug it directly into your speakers or use Bluetooth.)

- Make sure your mobile device can connect to your streaming media player.
- Have a friend record your performance, so you can show it later! (If you want to have video inception during your performance and are a little more tech-savvy, hook your streaming media player up to the projector in the performance space. During different parts of the performance, have a friend video either various audience members or the students during different parts of the performance for a cool effect!)
- You could also request the video from parents and family who attend, and then edit everything together.
- If your performance video needs editing, you can most likely do that on the device using apps like iMovie and FilmoraGo.
- Connect one of the devices up and make sure it operates on your streaming media player. (You will need to plug the device into the speaker system of your projector to hear the sound.)
- Set up a way for students to give their reactions to the performance, whether it be a worksheet, mobile device, or writing things out on the board.

During Class

- Open the video on your device and connect it to your streaming media player. (Make sure to connect your audio directly to the projector!)
  - Play the performance video and ask students to respond to it. Discuss and share thoughts afterward.
  - You could have your own little celebration movie party as students are watching.
  - Have discussion starters ready to help students reflect on their performance.
  - If you want to go a little further, you can share the performance video to student devices and ask them to use video editing software to cut out their favorite part or special moment of the concert. Make a montage of students' highlights.
- Record the students during class.
  - Use the camera app on your device to record students as they are performing or demonstrating mastery of a skill.
  - Once you have recorded the students, mirror your device to the screen and play the video. (With this activity you will not need to do any editing. It will be almost an immediate process from recording to viewing.)
  - Have students watch themselves and reflect on how they performed. This activity is great for observing posture, enunciation, playing techniques, and more.
- Have students create their performance.
  - With each teacher-created performance should come a student-created one. Get the students together in groups as soon as they enter the classroom.
  - Give them the instruction that they will be composing and arranging a body percussion piece that will have at least two parts played simultaneously.
  - Call two students to come up. Get your device out and mirror it to your board. Bring up a notation app such as Noteflight or QComposer in Quaver. Write a

rhythm on the bass line and have one student play it with body percussion. Write a rhythm or melody on the treble line and have the second student play or say it while the first student is still doing the rhythm.

o Have them play it together and record themselves. Ask students to reflect: were they as together as they thought they were?

o Pass out devices and ask the groups to do the same. Have at least two sections playing at the same time. Ask groups to record themselves performing and reflect. If they need to record again, have them re-record themselves.

o Ask each group to mirror their devices to the board using the Reflector app so you can have multiple devices up. Have each group play their video and reflect on it.

o As a fun bonus, try to play all the videos at the same time and see if any groups made similar sounds!

Assessment tip: Using the videos or audio recordings that you have created, ask students to reflect on their performance. You can have them discuss or orally reflect on their work. Another option would be to have students watch the video and complete a worksheet to reflect on what they did. An example worksheet is in Figure 6.5.

FIGURE 6.5 Worksheet example to use for activity (Photo Credit C. Dwinal)

GarageBand Activities

Recommended Grades: 3–6
Difficulty: Moderate
Time: 15–20 min.
Objective: Students will show an understanding of form and phrasing through composition using a looping tool.

Resources

- Streaming media player
- iPads
- Projector
- GarageBand app (WalkBand is a good alternative for Android but might not give you all the functionality you need for these activities.)

I love to have a few iPads in my room when I teach. They are great for doing small group work and sometimes large group work on the screen. The students enjoy having the power of being able to control the screen in their hands. With GarageBand, they can make studio-quality music quickly and easily and play interactive instruments. I use GarageBand

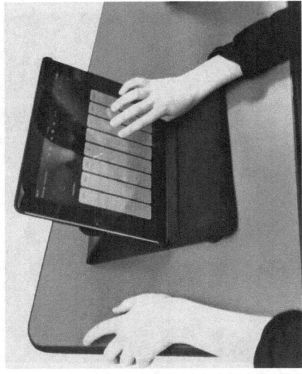

FIGURE 6.6 Students exploring Garageband on the iPad (Photo Credit C. Dwinal)

in many areas of my lessons. If I have a student who needs to be accommodated when playing an instrument, I set them up on an iPad with one of the interactive instruments in the app. Or sometimes I need a quick accompaniment track for a song we are learning so I can pull together a few layers of loops and play that while we perform. We can even use the instruments in my iPad band! There are many times when I bring out devices, and we make music just for the sake of making music. After we do these activities, I usually take the pieces they make and share them with the school community or edit them together for a portfolio.

Before Class

- Connect your streaming media player to your projector and make sure it works properly. (If you would like sound, you will need to plug the device directly into your speakers.)
- Make sure your mobile devices can connect to your streaming media player.
- Download the GarageBand app to your devices (or make sure your IT department has fulfilled your request for the app download).
- Right before class, make sure that your mobile devices have GarageBand on them and they are operating correctly.
- Connect one of the devices and make sure it operates on your streaming media player. (You will need to plug the iPad into the speaker system of your projector or use Bluetooth to hear the music.)

During Class

- Open GarageBand on one of the iPads and project it on to your screen.
  - Have the class help you create a quick piece of music. Use this time to teach students how to use the app.
  - The goal for this activity is to have students create a piece of music using just the loops in the GarageBand app in a round-robin "add to the story" game. They can do some editing, but they cannot delete any group member's addition to the piece.
  - Get students in groups of three to five. Hand each group one iPad and give them 10 minutes to complete the task. The first student needs to choose one loop and place it in the piece before passing it to the next person. The following person can either do some editing to the existing loop (change the length, change the placement, or adjust the effects) or add their own. Then they pass to the next person and so on until the 10 minutes are up. Everyone should have had at least one turn before the timer goes off.
  - Have each group project their piece onto to the board and play it for the class. Have them talk a little bit about their music as they present it.
- Get an afterschool iPad band going. Get Reflector going on your computer and have each student mirror their device onto the board.
  - Instruct each of them to bring up their instrument from the choices in the app.

- Get a steady beat loop going and have each student in the band practice keep the beat while watching the steady beat loop you have going.
  - Mix up the beats and start a "Follow the Leader" game that will work on a student's mastery of staying on the beat within an ensemble and works on their listening skills.
  - Get a notation app such as Noteflight on your device, and start by creating a line for each instrument. As a group, get the beat going before moving to the next steps of composing for the other instruments.
  - You can have the students playing the instruments create their line, or you can have the group as a whole compose the line for each digital instrument in the GarageBand app. Keep it simple because interactive instruments are a little more challenging to play compared to the traditional instrument.
  - Practice each line individually before putting them all together. Make sure to have a beat track going, to keep everyone together!
- Get a monthly podcast started! Make sure to mirror a device to your projector and bring up GarageBand. Watch a tutorial on how to make a podcast and work on it as a class before you have small groups continue throughout the year.
  - Assign a small group each month (or maybe a couple of students who are a little ahead of the class and need an extra challenge).
  - Give them a topic for their podcast. Suggestions include:
    - A recap of what they have been learning in music this month!
    - Composer/Music Artist of the Month
    - An audio drama based on a particular musical style or period in history
    - Research on a specific folk song they are learning
    - Have students play a song they are learning on their instruments
  - Have the group write up a script in either their document program or a notes app then send it to you for approval before the recording process starts.
  - When you give them the go-ahead:
    - Send them the approved copy of the script.
    - Give them an iPad with GarageBand (recommended that you have a mic that can plug into it for better sound. I have a Blue Snowflake mic for such occasions)
    - Give them a quiet space to record. You might need to have an agreement with another teacher in the building that allows students to go to their area, so the students have some supervision while they record.
  - Have them come back to the classroom after they have finished recording. Give students time to edit their podcast and add any special effects or music to it if they would like. Export the piece as an MP3 and have them email it to you.
  - Once complete, give it a listen and approve it. Upload it to a cloud-based sharing system like Google Drive, or if you want to get fancy, you can also do it on

SoundCloud where you can add it to a continuous playlist as you collect the podcasts.

- o Connect the device to the board and bring it up in GarageBand. Have the group come up to talk about the process, especially when it came to using the app, and reflect before having the class get comfy and listen. Discuss it afterward.
- o Share the podcast with teachers and administrators. Make it a monthly celebration! You can also play it from your device during an open house.

- Get an accompaniment track in literal minutes to go with any song or rap you are doing within class or rehearsal.
  - o Most of the boys that I taught in third grade and up had a love of rap music and beatboxing. I had one student who was also a very accomplished hip-hop dancer. There were several occasions when someone would come running up as soon as class started begging to share something new they just created. I would put GarageBand on the screen and pull together a quick beat to make their sharing session even better.
  - o During my ensemble rehearsals if I wanted to do a warm-up and we were rehearsing in a different part of the school where I was without my piano, I sometimes put together a quick accompaniment track in GarageBand while mirroring to the board. Most of the time, I had a heavy beat going on the track to keep the group together.
  - o If you are working on a piece of music on classroom instruments or a traditional folk song that does not have an accompaniment track, create one for it. You can add a new beat to an old favorite.

Assessment Tip: While students are in their small groups doing a round-robin composition, give them a specific form to follow. Then have them share their pieces with the class. Ask them to let the group know what form they were asked to follow and assess their work based on how they followed it.

Recorder Games

Recommended Grades: 3–6
Difficulty: Moderate
Time: 15–20 min.
Objective: Students will demonstrate proficiency in their recorder instrument by participating in class ensemble activities, and in small and large group activities.

Resources
- Streaming media player
- iPads or Android tablets

FIGURE 6.7 Getting some recorder practice in (Photo Credit C. Dwinal)

- Projector
- Photon Flash Browser
- http://www.joytunes.com/master/
- QuaverMusic.com

The recorder unit is always my favorite time of the year. I love bringing out the recorders and spending a whole term using the instruments in class. I found in my first year of teaching that I needed a variety of tools that were about the recorder to capture my students' attention and keep them excited. We do a range of centers, animated scores, and small group app work. When we use animated songs from Quaver, students are eager to play again and again. When we use the JoyTunes Recorder Master site, I find out how competitive my students are! Sometimes we play the games as a class, and sometimes we do small group work where they play in different corners of the room to try to beat the levels.

Before Class

- Connect your streaming media player to your projector and make sure it works properly. (If you would like sound, you will need to plug it directly into your speakers or use Bluetooth.)
- Make sure your mobile devices can connect to your streaming media player.

- These two resources are not apps to download; they are websites. Here is a trick to add a shortcut to a site on your home screen:
  - For Android tablets:
    - Go to your Internet browser and go to the website you would like to add to your home screen.
    - Tap the create bookmark icon.
    - When you are typing the information about your new bookmark, make sure you save it to your home screen!
  - For iPads
    - Open your Internet browser and go to the website you would like to add to your home screen.
    - Click the button down at the bottom that looks like a box with an arrow pointing up.
    - Scroll down until you see a button called "Add to home screen."
    - Title it and click "Add."
  - For JoyTunes, because it is still a Flash-based program, use a Flash-friendly browser app such as Photon Flash browser (downloadable from the app store).
- Test out each resource and make sure you have access to each. If you are going to use Quaver in small groups with students, they will need student access to log in.
- If you feel that you need some backup because you feel uncomfortable doing this by yourself right now, ask someone from your technology department or a technology coach to come in and help you get set up for this activity and then assist you while you are in the midst of the lesson.
- Test the microphone on the devices to make sure they pick up the instrument as it is playing.
- If you need to rent devices, make sure to do that before class. If you are a 1:1 school, ask students to bring their devices to class this day.
- Make sure that your mobile devices have the shortcuts or the Photon Flash browser app on them and they are operating correctly.
- Connect one of the devices up and make sure it communicates with your streaming media player. Connect the sound to your speaker system.
- Turn on JoyTunes and test it out with a recorder to make sure that it works properly.

During Class
- All of the interactive animations in Quaver are mobile device ready. Log in to the program and bring up the recorder songs that are in Quaver's ClassPlay.
  - First, use the fingering chart to practice the notes they will find in the song. (Have a student lead this activity by coming up and modeling the notes the class need to practice, and leading the group in long tones or other warm-ups.)
  - Bring up the Recorder Olympics screen and point to different melodies having students play each one. If they are ready for the next step, play one of the

background tracks at a quicker tempo. You can change the level of difficulty in the melody as well by choosing either bronze, silver, or gold.

- o Bring up the animated score for the song you would like the students to play. These animated screens also highlight the notes so you can step away from the screen after hitting Play and sit with your students to participate with them (a great way to enjoy the learning with your class!)
- o If you would like students to play in small groups, make sure that they have student access or an access code to log in.
  - Divide the students into small groups (probably no more than four per group).
  - Give each group a mobile device and instructions on how to access the animated scores.
  - Have them open the songs and practice together while you walk around the room and facilitate.
- In JoyTunes, the game is controlled by how your students play their instrument. Make sure you have it up on the Photon Flash browser app, where it will work the best.
  - o When you bring up the game, it will ask to play a specific note to get started. Play that note together and make sure you focus on matching pitch. If you need to practice, you might need to pause and play the note on the piano and focus on this for a while. Matching pitch is the most important thing for this activity.
  - o Press Play and follow the instructions on the screen. Students have to make sure they keep pitch, stay on the beat, and adhere to the dynamics while using good breath support.
  - o If you would like students to play in small groups, make sure that they have a device that can access JoyTunes.
    - Divide the students into small groups (no more than four per group).
    - Give each group a mobile device and instructions on how to access the game.
    - Have them play the games together.

Assessment Tip: Assess students by observing them while they play in an ensemble together (small or large group). Have student volunteers come up and lead the class while you wander from group to group listening and watching. You can also video students as they play to assess later or have students doing small group work and call up one student at a time to play for you.

MadPad

Recommended Grades: 3–7
Difficulty: Moderate
Time: 15-40 min.

Objective: Students will make connections between what they are learning in music class and future careers through creation of a found sounds product during class.

Resources

- Streaming media player
- iPads or Android tablets
- Projector
- MadPad by Smule App

I discovered the MadPad app after doing a found sounds unit some years back. Students have the freedom to go out in the classroom, the playground, or the rest of the school to find new sounds and sample them into the app to create a new piece of music. They always have so much fun exploring and finding new sounds. When they find out it is a form of sampling that DJs do, they get very excited. It also is a great way to introduce students to being Foley artists. Have them find sounds that meet specific criteria like the sound like someone walking, a bone breaking, someone crying, and so on. We use them for found sounds compositions or score silent movies for a project. It's a great sampling tool!

Before Class

- Connect your streaming media player to your projector and make sure it works properly. (If you would like sound, you will need to plug the device directly into your speakers.)
- Make sure your mobile devices can connect to your streaming media player.
- Explore the app yourself before you use it in your lesson. When you are familiar with it, create your sampling board from different sounds that you can find around the school. Then you can use this as an example for your students.
- Make sure that your mobile devices have the MadPad app on them and they are operating correctly. (Or make sure your IT department has fulfilled your request for the app download.)
- If you need to rent devices, make sure to sign up before class. If you are a 1:1 school, remind your students to bring their devices for this activity.
- On the day of class, connect one of the devices up and make sure it operates on your streaming media player. Connect the sound to your speaker system to make sure you can hear the noises.

During Class

- The first activity you can do is a great way to end a found sounds unit or to teach students about how a DJ samples music for their mixes.
  - On the board, bring up the MadPad app and show students the sample board that you created beforehand. Demonstrate for them how you created music with it.

- o Show students how you start a new board and add sounds to it. Have a few volunteers come up to help create the board with the class.
- o Have a discussion relating it to real life. How do DJs get those unique sounds that are not familiar instruments we all know?
- o Break the students up into small groups (no more than four to a group).
- o Give them each a mobile device, time, and a space to explore and fill up their sample boards. Make sure you get permission if you want students go beyond your classroom door to discover new sounds.
- o Have them come back and share what they found and improvise a new piece of music with the sounds they have discovered.
- The next activity could go along with a discussion on Foley artists.
  - o Open the MadPad app on the projector and show students the sample board that you created. Demonstrate for them how you would add sounds to a silent animated movie clip.
  - o Show students how you start a new board and add sounds to it. Have a few volunteers help create the board for the class.
  - o Have a discussion relating it to real life. How do Foley artists recreate daily sounds we hear with other objects?
  - o Break the students up into small groups (no more than four to a group).
  - o Give them a list of sounds they need to recreate:
    - People walking
    - A bone breaking
    - Someone yelling from a distance
    - A door closing
    - Someone laughing
    - A high five
    - Someone scratching their head
    - Wind blowing
    - Clothing rustling
  - o Give them each a mobile device, time, and a space to explore and fill up their sample boards. Make sure you get permission if you want students go beyond your classroom door to discover new sounds.
  - o Find a silent clip library where students can choose their clips. Have them download them to the movie editor on another device. Have them record their own sounds as needed.
  - o Have students come back together as a group and share using the streaming media player system to play their clips from their devices. Then they can explain the sounds that they used.

Assessment Tip: Assess students on their final presentation/performance to the class and final MadPad board choices. You could videotape their presentations to assess later. This activity could be a self-reflection assessment opportunity as well.

StaffWars

Recommended Grades: 4–12
Difficulty: Beginner
Time: 10–30 min.
Objective: Students will demonstrate knowledge of identifying notes and rests on the staff at a rapid-fire pace.

Resources
- Streaming media player
- iPads or Android tablets
- Projector
- StaffWars app (found on App Store or Google Play Store)

StaffWars is a popular app that has been around as a software program for quite some time. Now a mobile app, students can use it on their devices at home or on the go. Gamifying the task of learning note names and rests helps take the process of memorizing this musical language to a whole different level. A lot of my students compare it to a popular sci-fi movie franchise of a similar name!

Before Class
- Connect your streaming media player to your projector and make sure it works properly. (If you would like sound, you will need to plug your device directly into your speakers or use Bluetooth.)
- Make sure your mobile devices can connect to your streaming media player.
- Download the StaffWars app to your devices (or make sure your IT department has fulfilled your request for the app download).
- On the day of class, make sure that your mobile devices have StaffWars on them and they are operating correctly.
- Connect one of the devices up and make sure it operates on your streaming media player.

During Class
- Use one of the mobile devices connected to your board and have students volunteer answers to help you defeat the note-shaped attackers.
  - Have students shout out the answers when you are playing. Take the solution that you hear first.
    - If you do not want the class shouting out what they think the answers are, come up with different moves for the different answers on the screen. Take the solution that corresponds to the movement that most students are doing.

- Next, pass the tablet to student volunteers to take turns answering three or four answers each as fast as they can before moving to the next volunteer. Keep it on the screen to allow other students in the room to see. The slower a student answers, the harder it will be for the next person!
  - Get students in a big circle. Explain that they can only answer a certain number of questions before passing the device to the next person in the circle. If they answer more than the allotted questions then they will not have a turn next round.
  - Go around the circle until everyone has had a turn. (You might need to restart the game once or twice.)
  - A variation of this: Keep the circle but have students answer until they can't answer a question before they pass it on to the next person! The person who can get the most questions correct after everyone has taken their turn wins!
  - Another variation of this: Keep the controls of this program to yourself. Make a circle if you have the room; if not, you can do this in rows. Start with one student and ask them to identify the answer on the board. If they get it right, they get to start the game. If they get it wrong, then you keep going around until you find one student who gets it correct. The first student who got the right answer stands behind or next to the next student. The first one to answer the question on the board correctly gets to move on. If the student who got the last question successfully gets the next one wrong, they have to sit in that student's chair or stand in their spot and the student who got it correct moves forward. This activity is basically a simple game of "Around the World" with a fast-paced tool. (If it gets too fast and things and start to collapse, keep it fun and let it be a learning experience.)
- When students have been adequately introduced to the game, take it to the next level:
  - Pass out the tablets to either individuals or small groups and have them play the game. The highest score takes the win!
  - If you use an app like Reflector 3, you can have students mirror multiple devices to the screen so the class can see everyone as they compete to get the highest score. To mirror an iPad, all you have to do is:
    - Swipe up while on the home screen.
    - Click Mirror and select the device you want to mirror to.
    - To mirror an Android device, you will need a third-party app like Reflector 3 to make it easy. Chromebooks can use devices like Chromecast to reflect, but Reflector 3 works as well.

Assessment Tip: StaffWars will give students a score based on how many they got right. Ask students to get what they feel is their best score and submit it to you. You can assign this to them as a pre- and post-test for a music theory unit.

Drum Machine Accompaniment

Recommended Grades: 4–12

Difficulty: Moderate

Time: 15–20 min.

Objective: Students will demonstrate proficiency in song composition using digital creation tools.

Resources

- Streaming media player
- iPads or Android tablets
- Projector
- DM1 app or Launchpad app.

Giving students a look into a sequencer or drum machine shows them another world where DJs and producers create beats. This lesson can spark their passion for a career in music. I have some students who are not really interested in a lot of the things we do in music, but when we start using tools like these, they jumped right in because they the

FIGURE 6.8 Working on their compositions (Photo Credit C. Dwinal)

relevance to musical styles they loved to listen to outside of school. Seeing how they can create and compose music they like gives them the motivation to continue doing it outside of class. I have students download the apps after we used them in class and periodically come in and show me what they created to go along with their skating videos and funny YouTube sketches.

Before Class

- Connect your streaming media player to your projector and make sure it works properly. (If you would like sound, you will need to plug the device directly into your speakers or use Bluetooth.)
- Make sure your mobile devices can connect to your streaming media player.
- Download the DM1 or Launchpad apps to your devices. (Or make sure your IT department has fulfilled your request for the app download.)
- Play with the apps before you do this activity so you are familiar with them enough to demonstrate them to your students. Come up with a few examples to show them for class. YouTube has some great demonstrations for these apps; you can show them to your students.
- On the day of class, make sure that your mobile devices have the DM1 or Launchpad apps on them and they are operating correctly.
- Connect one of the devices and make sure it operates on your streaming media player. (You will need to plug the device into the speaker system of your projector to hear the music.)
- If you feel uncomfortable with doing this activity, make sure to ask someone from your tech department to come to your room to help you.

During Class

- For this activity, you will need to give students a walkthrough of the app that they will be using. Play the introductory video by mirroring it to the board for the class to see.
- Give them the goal of this activity: To write a short song based on a specific topic of choice and create an accompaniment track to go along with it.
- The checkpoints for this activity are:
  - Choose a topic for this piece.
  - Write lyrics for that song and practice saying and playing your piece.
  - Play with the DM1 app and get familiar with it.
  - Build a beat that will work for your lyrics.
  - Practice the song together with the lyrics and the melody.
  - Perform it for the class.
- Choose a topic for the songs that students will be composing. It can be anything from favorite sports to current events. Have each student choose a different theme within specific criteria.

- Tell them that they will be making beats on the app, and they must have an A section and a B section, followed by a return to the A section. They will also be writing lyrics for this piece on the topic they chose.
- Give students some insight as to what careers these sorts of apps can be used in, such as DJing and being an audio engineer.
- Break them into small groups or have them do this by themselves. Pass out devices so they can use an app, or have them use a pencil and paper.
- Ask students to work on the lyrics first before putting a beat to it. Walk around the room to help students as they are working.
- Have them mirror their music on the board using the streaming media player and perform their song for the class.

Assessment Tip: Assess students on their final performance to the class along with their final mix.

News Crew

Recommended Grades: 5–12
Difficulty: Expert
Time: 1 to 2 class periods
    Objective: Students will write and produce a short news show on a specific musical topic to demonstrate an understanding of the subject.

Resources
- Streaming media player
- iPads or Android tablet
- Projector
- Green screen fabric
- Set dressing and costumes for the news set
- Microphone (preferably one that hooks into one of your devices. I usually prefer a Snowball or Snowflake microphone from Blue microphones with a USB adaptor.)
- iMovie/FilmoraGo apps
- Audio Recorder app or Audacity on a computer
- Do Ink app

Mobile devices have made it so much easier to be able to create projects that we once thought were out of our reach. With all of the bad news going around in the world, having students report on the positive things in the world to the school community can be crucial. To bring this into the music realm, have students collect all the information that they can on a concept you are teaching and report on it as a news story. Have them report on Wagner's new opera, or the history of hip-hop.

Before Class

- Connect your streaming media player to your projector and make sure it works properly. (If you would like sound, you will need to plug it directly into your speakers or use Bluetooth.)
- Make sure your mobile devices can connect to your streaming media player.
- Download the iMovie/Filmora Go and Do Ink apps to your devices (Or make sure your IT department has fulfilled your request for the app download.)
- You will need to build a small green screen area. Green cloth or art paper can do the trick! Find a table or desk that can serve as a news desk (or you can put a student in charge of putting the set together).
- Get familiar with iMovie/FilmoraGo and Do Ink apps. You will need to give students a tutorial on how to create these apps so be familiar enough with the program to show them what you would like them to do.
- Students will need prerequisite knowledge of the topic they will be reporting on, so this would be the perfect end-of-the-unit activity.
- You might need students a few minutes more than just the regular class period. Clear it with the classroom teacher first before you continue with the activity.
- Find a few examples of news reporting shows to show students.
- Create a list of goals and checkpoints to guide students through this project before you jump in because it is a fast-paced activity. Goal list can be:
  - Assign tasks to everyone in the group (Depending on your class size, you might only have one or two groups). You will need at least:
    - Two anchorpersons
    - Two field reporters
    - Two or three camera people
    - At least one audio person
    - Researchers
    - Scriptwriters
    - Editors
    - Set dressers and makeup people
  - Give students a short list of topics they can report on. Examples could include
    - Composers and what they get caught doing in their day to day lives. (Make it a TMZ moment!)
    - *Behind the Music*–style video. Have the group pick a music style and deconstruct it by talking about the influencers and music that defines it, and what makes that style of music what it is.
    - How to write a song. Report on the different parts of a song, from identifying notes and rests, to putting them on the staff, to adding in dynamics and tempo.

- o Create goals for the groups to meet for this activity.
  - Create a 5- to 10-minute news show about a particular musical topic.
  - Choose a topic and assign roles.
  - Research facts and write a script.
  - Decorate the set and find costumes for on-air talent.
  - Learn how to use the audio and video tools.
  - Get approval for the script from the teacher.
  - Run through a rehearsal and get ready on set.
  - Film everything that they need on the green screen.
  - Edit video footage.
  - Edit audio and do any voice-overs that are needed.
  - Put the whole thing together.
  - Watch it and share it with others!
  - o Make sure you have collected all the materials students will need for this activity.
- On the day of class, get all the materials that students will need for this activity.
- If you need to rent devices out for this activity, request them from your technology department. You will only need a few. If you are a 1:1 school ask students to bring their devices.
- Put all the digital resources you need for this activity on the board.

During Class

- Introduce the goal: To create a news broadcast that reports on a crucial music topic.
- Show them some examples of news broadcasts featuring kids from a video sharing service like YouTube.
- Discuss what the expectations are for the next couple of classes and answer any questions the students may have.
- Break students up into groups if your class is large. If not, you could probably do this as a whole class activity.
- Have them choose a topic and start researching it. Have the researchers write down facts about the subject to flesh out the script.
- While the researchers are still working, have the scriptwriters start on the script while they receive facts from the researchers.
- The anchorpersons and field reporters can work with the scriptwriters to have input on what will work best with them on the screen.
- Get the audio and camera people getting familiar with the programs. Have them go through tutorials and create examples to be well-practiced as they are getting ready for showtime.
- Have the editors learn Do Ink for green screen editing.
- When the script is complete, have the writers present it to you for approval.
- Once you have approved the script, run through a quick rehearsal before getting the onscreen talent dressed up and in place. You might have other places where you put the field reports.

- Get the camera and audio people ready. Have the scriptwriters and researchers on hand to help with any script revisions or fact-checking.
- Start filming. They might have to film the desk scenes first and then do the field reporters in front of the green screen.
- Have the editors start editing the video footage first while audio makes sure to get any extra voice-overs needed for the piece.
- Add the audio and video together and make any final edits.
- Show the final product to the class! Then have them reflect on and discuss the final product.
- Make sure to share the final product with the school community. If you can, make a new episode every month!
   - A variation on this would be to have small teams of students write a 2- to 3-minute video script on a specific part of the topic for a breaking news bulletin. It should be a shorter video. It could be a quick news story about one particular composer, or have them report on one specific song or current artist. You could put a reporter in front of the green screen to report, as if they are in the field.

Assessment Tip: Assess the group on their final product, paying close attention to the creativity, content, collaboration, and organization of the overall video.

Virtual Field Trip

Recommended Grades: 6–12
Difficulty: Expert
Time: 1 to 2 class periods
Objective: Students will create a virtual reality experience to display their knowledge of their researched culture.

Resources
- Streaming media player
- iPod Touches/smartphones and laptops
- Projector
- Google Expeditions and CoSpaces Edu
- Google Cardboard

I have been fascinated with augmented reality (AR) and virtual reality (VR) since I first saw demos of them years ago. Students hold the mobile device over the word and see the AR come to life on the screen, explaining the meaning of the word. When Google and

FIGURE 6.9 Students were always fascinated with new innovations like AR and VR (Photo Credit C. Dwinal)

CoSpaces Edu came onto the scene, they made VR more accessible to education. Now with Apple's AI, teachers can take each student beyond the classroom walls and show them parts of the world that they may never see in real life. It is a way to increase the interactivity and student engagement in the instruction and take students beyond the four walls of your classroom, making a significant impact on their education.

Before Class
- This activity would be perfect as a follow-up to learning about a specific song from a different country or a great final project for a world music unit.
- Connect your streaming media player to your projector and make sure it works properly. (If you would like sound, you will need to plug it directly into your speakers or use Bluetooth.)
- Make sure your mobile devices can connect to your streaming media player.
- Download the Google Expeditions and CoSpaces Edu apps to your devices. (Or make sure your IT department has fulfilled your request for the app download.)
- If you cannot get access to iPod Touches, ask students to download the Google Expeditions app to their smartphones to be used during class only.

- You will need to acquire Google Cardboard viewers for this project if you do not have a lot of funds to purchase a set. Places like DonorsChoose.org would be a great way to raise funds. Keep in mind that you can use these over and over again for different VR activities. You could also put in a request for a few iPod Touches or old smartphones for this activity.
- Get familiar with CoSpaces Edu and build an example for students to see so they know what is expected of them.
- Sign up for Google Expeditions and learn how to be a guide.
- If you need some assistance for this activity, ask your technology department to help you during class.
- Share your objective for this activity and the activities they will need to do to reach the final goal.
  - Objective: To create a virtual reality experience to demonstrate your knowledge of the culture we are studying.
    - Experience a digital field trip using Google Expeditions as a class.
    - Collect at least five facts about the culture.
    - Build a VR experience to show the class displaying these five facts.
    - Present it to the class.
- On the day of class, make sure that your mobile devices have Google Expeditions on them and that they are operating correctly.
- Double-check that you have CoSpaces Edu on the individual devices, and that it is working correctly.
- Connect one of the devices and make sure it operates on your streaming media player.
- Connect to Google Expeditions and make sure that the Google Cardboard viewer is put together and easily accessible for students.
- If students are learning a song, make sure they have already practiced it, and prepare the class to practice it one more time.

During Class

- When students arrive in class, begin a discussion about what the expectations will be for the next couple of classes.
- Practice the song they have been learning to get it fresh in their memory.
- Pass out Google Cardboard viewers and have students cue up the Google Expeditions app. Guide them through a local field trip as an example.
- Give students a refresher on how to use CoSpaces Edu.
- Cue up your example on the board and show it to the group.
- Explain when the project is due and that they will all present during the same class.
- Share the goal and checklist with students and have them get out their devices to begin creating their interactive experience.

- Give students time to apply the knowledge they have been learning in class to their work. Circulate the room to guide and answer any questions they may have as they are working on the project.
- While students are working on their assignments, have them sign up for a time slot on the day of presentations.
- When students are working, make sure to play a recording of the song they are learning in the background, as inspiration.
- On presentation day, practice the song again before presentations start. Have students come up to the board to show the class their experiences and share their facts.
- Put students' experiences into the Google Cardboard viewers. Have them discover each other's work.
  - Put out a display for Open House night to show families and administration what students have been doing.

Assessment Tip: Assess students on their final product and how well they demonstrated the facts and explained it to their classmates.

History of Rock 'n' Roll

Recommended Grades: 8–12
Difficulty: Expert
Time: 2 to 3 class periods
Objective: Students will create a 5-minute video that demonstrates knowledge of the music from a chosen musical decade using green screen effects and video editing software.

Resources
- Media
- iPads
- Projector
- Green screen
- iMovie
- Do Ink

I was student teaching at a local high school. My cooperating teacher, who was a seasoned veteran and on his way to retiring soon, had his whole curriculum down pat. One of the classes he taught was History of Rock 'n' Roll. I had never experienced a course like this before. It was so much fun to watch him speak to his students on the music of the 1960s and 1970s. Imagine taking a class like this, and have students immerse themselves into the periods that they are learning: when the Beatles first played a public concert, or Woodstock. They can take all they learn and share their knowledge with the class.

FIGURE 6.10 To keep the peace in class when working on digital compositions, headphones were always ready. I would let older students bring their earbuds in to use on these days too (Photo Credit C. Dwinal)

Before Class

- This activity would be excellent to do at the end of a unit about the history of rock 'n' roll or a music history course.
- Connect your streaming media player to your projector and make sure it works properly. (If you would like sound, you will need to plug the device directly into your speakers or use Bluetooth.)
- Make sure your mobile devices can connect to your streaming media player.
- Download the iMovie and Do Ink apps to your devices. (Or make sure your IT department has fulfilled your request for the app download.)
- You will need to build a small green screen area. Green cloth or art paper can do the trick!
- Get familiar with iMovie and Do Ink and build an example for students to see so they understand expectations.
- If you need some assistance for this activity, ask your technology department to help you during class.
- Create your objective for this activity and the activities they will need to do to reach the goal.

- o Objective: You must create a 5-minute video that demonstrates knowledge of a musical decade using green screen effects to put yourself into the significant events of the period.
  - Choose one decade and research the top five leading artists of the period. Find the top three events that shaped the music of the era. Discover what the primary genre of music that was popular, and any other specific facts that were special about the decade.
  - Create a storyboard for your video.
  - Create a script for your video.
  - Practice your video and film it.
  - You must have at least part of the video filmed in front of the green screen.
  - Edit and cut your video together.
  - Choose specific audio clips from the music of the era to add to your video as final touches.
  - Export your project and email it to your teacher.
- On the day of class, make sure that your mobile devices have Do Ink and iMovie on them and they are operating correctly.
- If you are not a 1:1 school, make sure you rent out devices for this activity.
- Connect one of the devices and make sure it operates on your streaming media player.
- Make sure the green screen area is set up and ready to go.
- Ask students to bring headphones if possible.

During Class
- When students arrive in class, begin a discussion about what the expectations will be for the next couple of classes.
- Give a quick refresher on what they have been learning in each decade. Post a Google Doc of the review to give students a visual.
- Give students a refresher on how to use iMovie if needed. If they have never used it before, then you will need to give them a quick tutorial.
- Give students a quick tutorial on how to use Do Ink, so they know how to use it. They will need to know the Green Screen side of the app.
- Cue up your example on the board and show it to the group.
- Explain when the project is due and that they will all present during the same class.
- Share the goal and checklist with students and have them get out their devices to begin researching and mapping out their videos.
- Give students time to apply the knowledge they have been learning in class to their work. Circulate the room to guide and answer any questions they may have as they are working on the project. Make sure the students map and block out what they are going to do before they start filming.
- While students are working on their assignment, have them sign up for a presentation slot.

- Make sure students get a piece of their video on the green screen. The rest of the video can be filmed with any other background. Students can create or acquire any props, costumes, or any other background that they might want to use.
- Once students have collected their clips, they will need to edit and provide voice-over for their overall project. They will need headphones for this and a quiet area to do their editing, perhaps in another room.
- Once students are ready with their project, they will need to export their full video. Then they will need to share it with you by emailing it, or you could set up a shared Google Drive folder for students to save their creations.
  - You'll need to have their email addresses so you can send them the shared link.
  - Go to your Google Drive and click New in the upper left corner.
  - Select Folder and name your new folder.
  - Click the person icon in the upper right-hand corner to adjust sharing settings.
  - Then, you can either get the shareable link and send it out to students or share with a specific class email group.
  - Students then can drag and drop their creations to the folder for you to access anytime and anywhere.
- When students have completed their projects, bring them together as a class, and have a presentation day. They must come up to share their work from a device and project it onto the board via streaming media player.
  - Ask students to introduce their short video, including what decade they chose.
  - Have them play the video.
  - Ask them to give a one- to two-sentence reflection on their process for the project.
  - Take all students' projects after you have graded them and put them into a reel to send to administrators, as a way to show what students have been learning.

Assessment Tip: Assess students on their final video, paying close attention to creativity, content, and organization.

7

Resources Index

The following are apps, websites, and software mentioned in this book. Apps can be located through an App Store or Google Play search by title.

Apps
MadPad

- Recommended Grades: 3–7
- Level: Intermediate-Advanced
- Price: Free for all
- Tags: Mobile Device, Streaming Media Player, General, Critical Thinking, Creating, Career
- Description: MadPad is a creative composing app that allows students to sample different sounds by videorecording short clips and creating a sample board. Then it enables the user to click on the various videos on the board to play the sounds, similar to a DJ drum machine.

Metaverse

- Recommended Grades: 4–12
- Level: Advanced
- Price: Based on product
- Tags: Mobile Device, Streaming Media Player, General, Critical Thinking, Creating, Augmented Reality
- Description: Metaverse is an AR tool that is mostly free for teachers. Create targets that could be anything from 3D models to videos, and then students can see the targets by pointing their device at specific objects. This app is a great way to add a level of interactivity to posters and other visuals in your room.

Interactive Visual Ideas for Musical Classroom Activities. Catherine Dwinal, Oxford University Press (2020). © Oxford University Press.
DOI: 10.1093/oso/9780190929855.001.0001

Guitar Elite-Chord Play Center

- Recommended Grades: 2–8
- Level: Beginner-Intermediate
- Price: In-app purchases
- Tags: Mobile Device, Streaming Media Player, General, Instrumental, Playing, Ensembles, Modifications
- Description: A simple guitar app that has different styles of the instrument. Choose the guitar, and then you can choose the chords and strum along to demonstrate certain chord progressions or accompany a short tune with your students. Students could also use an app like this to create their music and play along to it, especially if they do not have access to a guitar at that moment.

Notability

- Recommended Grades: 2–12
- Level: Beginner-Expert
- Price: Free for all
- Tags: Projector, Streaming Media Player, iPad, General, Utilities, Mobile Devices, PDF Editor
- Description: A notes app that allows the user to type or write using a finger or stylus, or even insert pictures directly into the note itself. Students could use this to take notes. Users can then organize the notes in the way that they desire and be able to go back and refer to them later or export and share with others.

Evernote

- Recommended Grades: K–12
- Level: Beginner-Expert
- Price: Based on product
- Tags: Projector, Streaming Media Player, iPads, General, Utilities, Website, Cloud-Based
- Description: A notes app that can carry across all user devices. Take notes, import pictures, and organize everything you need to remember into a system that will work for you. Other tools in Evernote include a web clipper, scanned documents, and a way to tag all of your resources to find them easily later on.

Plickers

- Recommended Grades: 3–12
- Level: Beginner-Advanced
- Price: Free for all
- Tags: Projector, Streaming Media Player, General, Assessment, Mobile Devices
- Description: An assessment tool that allows educators to create quizzes for students. The teacher hands out specialized cards to each student. When the teacher asks a

question, students hold their cards up to a certain way, and the teacher scans the cards with the app to collect the answers. This app only requires one device to complete the assessments.

Keynote
- Recommended Grades: PreK–12
- Level: Beginner-Advanced
- Price: Free
- Tags: Projector, Wi-Fi, PowerPoint, Streaming Media Player, iPad
- Description: Like PowerPoint but iPad-friendly. This app has the power to create a presentation right on your device that you can use for daily lessons.

Cleartune
- Recommended Grades: 4–12
- Level: Beginner-Advanced
- Price: $3.99
- Tags: Mobile Device, Streaming Media Player, General, Instrumental, Playing, Ensembles, Utilities
- Description: A tuning app that allows students and teachers alike to have an accurate chromatic tuner readily available from their phones or devices. It takes away the hassle of having to remember and carry around an extra device.

Amazing Slow Downer
- Recommended Grades: 4–12
- Level: Beginner-Advanced
- Price: $14.99
- Tags: Mobile Device, Streaming Media Player, General, Instrumental, Playing, Ensembles, Utilities
- Description: You can take pretty much any song that you are practicing and slow it down to a more reasonable pace to work on it. You can also change pitch and loop the piece to get the most out of your rehearsal.

Easy Xylophone
- Recommended Grades: 3–12
- Level: Beginner-Advanced
- Price: Based on product
- Tags: Mobile Device, Streaming Media Player, General, Instrumental, Playing, Ensembles, Modifications
- Description: A xylophone app that acts similar to the real thing. An alternative to the real deal if you do not have enough for the class, or want to mix things up

a bit in your ensemble with a little traditional and a little digital. May be a good alternative for students with differing abilities who are unable to use traditional instruments.

Hand Drums
- Recommended Grades: 3–12
- Level: Beginner-Advanced
- Price: Based on product
- Tags: Mobile Device, Streaming Media Player, General, Instrumental, Playing, Ensembles, Differentiation
- Description: A simple interactive instrument app that allows the user to tap the drums instead of physically playing them. Perfect for teachers who don't have enough instruments but can grab a few extra devices from the media center to add some color. Teachers also can use apps like this as a modification for students who have differing physical abilities and need something a little different to be a part of the class ensemble.

Virtuoso Piano
- Recommended Grades: 3–12
- Level: Beginner-Advanced
- Price: Based on product
- Tags: Mobile Device, Streaming Media Player, General, Instrumental, Playing, Ensembles, Modifications
- Description: A great and straightforward piano app. I use it occasionally during choir rehearsals and excursions outside of my room where I don't have immediate access to a piano and need something simple for warm-ups. Students can also use this app to learn necessary keyboarding skills if they do not have a real keyboard.

Piano Maestro
- Recommended Grades: 2–6
- Level: Beginner-Intermediate
- Price: Based on product
- Tags: Mobile Device, Streaming Media Player, General, Instrumental, Performing, Piano
- Description: Made by the same company that created the JoyTunes recorder app. Piano Maestro is an instructional tool that teaches students how to play the piano in a game-like situation. They can use either the in-game piano or a real piano. This app also has a large variety of popular songs that engage students at all levels. I use this app with a few of my beginning piano students as a reward, and it motivates them to continue to practice.

Ukeoke

- Recommended Grades: 4–12
- Level: Beginner-Intermediate
- Price: Free with in-app purchases
- Tags: Mobile Device, Streaming Media Player, General, Instrumental, Playing, Ensembles, Ukulele, Projector
- Description: A ukulele resource that offers beginner playing tools along with popular and current songs in a play-along format. This app includes vibrant and engaging visual tools for full class jamming or at-home individual practice. Everything is broken down into simple chunks that allow newbies to seasoned veterans of the instrument to enjoy playing.

Toca Band

- Recommended Grades: PreK–5
- Level: Beginner
- Price: Free
- Tags: Mobile Device, Streaming Media Player, General, Instrumental, Playing, Ensembles, Modifications

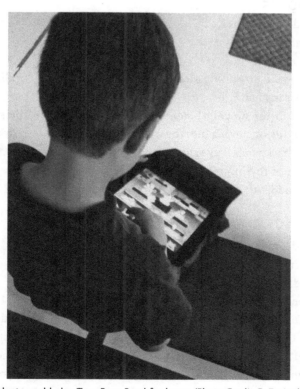

FIGURE 7.1 My students could play Toca Boca Band for hours (Photo Credit C. Dwinal)

- Description: Toca Boca was voted the number one app for children with autism in 2012. Toca Band is a fun and straightforward music creation app that can keep students engaged for hours. Students drag and drop characters into different levels of the stage to create a composition. Each level gives each character a separate loop of music to jam out. When students put a character in the star, they can improvise their own melody!

Reflector 3
- Recommended Grades: PreK–12
- Level: Beginner-Advanced
- Price: $14.99
- Tags: Projector, Wi-Fi, Bluetooth, Mobile Devices, Mirroring
- Description: One of the top device mirroring programs on the market. Allows several different types of devices to connect to your computer and show what is on the screen. Imagine having several different iPads all up on your board at once while students are competing or collaborating. Using the power of Bluetooth, you can connect any device, from an iPad to a Chromebook, to your computer, and project its screen right onto your desktop.

Singing Fingers
- Recommended Grades: PreK–2
- Level: Beginner
- Price: $0.99
- Tags: Mobile Device, Streaming Media Player, General, Singing, Audio Recording, Art Connection, Assessment
- Description: With the Singing Fingers app, students draw on the screen with their finger while talking or singing into the microphone. When they redraw what is on the screen, it plays back what they said or sang. This app is perfect for students to reflect on their singing or rhythm reading skills. I love to have my younger kiddos sing and draw a solfège ladder to demonstrate competency of matching pitch.

Doceri
- Recommended Grades: PreK–12
- Level: Beginner-Advanced
- Price: Free with in-app purchases
- Tags: Projector, Wi-Fi, Bluetooth, Mobile Devices, Remote Desktop
- Description: Imagine feeling stuck at the front of the room with a desktop computer and projector tethering you up there. With Doceri, you can connect a mobile device to your computer and go wireless while still controlling what is on the screen. You can also use it as an interactive whiteboard slate, or do screen captures your instruction. It turns your device into an ultimate tool to help you with your daily instruction!

Splashtop
- Recommended Grades: PreK–12
- Level: Beginner-Advanced
- Price: Based on product
- Tags: Projector, Wi-Fi, Bluetooth, Mobile Devices, Remote Desktop
- Description: Splashtop is a high powered remote desktop app that puts a user's desktop on their mobile device to control from anywhere in the room or school! It is a cheaper alternative to an interactive board and allows you to be anywhere in the room while still engaging the class. You also can have students manipulate what is on the board from their seat.

iDoceo
- Recommended Grades: PreK–12
- Level: Beginner-Advanced
- Price: $11.99
- Tags: Assessment, Utilities, iPad, Streaming Media Player, Attendance, Planning, Grading
- Description: The ultimate teacher tool for educators. This one is catered toward arts education because it is customizable and has so many tools that can be incorporated. Use it as a grade book, a seating chart tool, and even a planner.

Musicnotes Decks: Music Flash Cards
- Recommended Grades: 2–9
- Level: Beginner
- Price: Free
- Tags: Streaming Media Player, iPad, Music Theory, Games, Whole Class, Small Group
- Description: Take the deck of physical classroom music theory flashcards you use in your teaching and make them digital. Use them with small groups and large groups alike to help students learn the different musical symbols and notes and rests.

DM1
- Recommended Grades: 7–12
- Level: Intermediate-Advanced
- Price: $4.99
- Tags: Mobile Device, Streaming Media Player, General, Instrumental, Playing, Audio Mixing, Career
- Description: This app is more of an advanced music creation tool that turns your mobile device into an expensive drum machine. Endless options of loops and audio manipulation tools let users adjust the audio in the music they are creating as it is playing. Students get a taste of being a DJ or audio engineer as they learn how to make beats on their mobile devices.

Bebot

- Recommended Grades: PreK–3
- Level: Beginner
- Price: $1.99
- Tags: Mobile Device, Streaming Media Player, General, Instrumental, Playing, Synthesizer
- Description: An easy to use music-making tool that allows users to experience a full keyboard in a touch control system built into the shape of a cute robot. This robot is a powerful synthesizer in disguise used by beginners and professional musicians alike.

Launchpad

- Recommended Grades: 6–12
- Level: Intermediate-Advanced
- Price: Based on product
- Tags: Mobile Device, Streaming Media Player, General, Instrumental, Playing, Audio Mixing, Careers
- Description: Launchpad is a music mixing app by the company Novation that gives students a small taste of making beats, editing audio, and sequencing. Students can choose from a wide variety of loops with no fear of mixing beats. They can learn about the different layers in the music they listen to daily.

My Singing Monsters

- Recommended Grades: PreK–2
- Level: Beginner
- Price: Based on product
- Tags: Projector, Streaming Media Player, Streaming Media Player, iPad, Android Tablet, General, Creating, Ostinatos
- Description: An app that takes users to another world with monsters that each have a different vocal ostinato. Students can grow different monsters and create whole ensembles singing together to make different musical creations. Students can watch their little monsters grow and evolve, feed them, and layer them together to form various small choirs. Users can also have multiple worlds to create several different pieces.

Blob Chorus

- Recommended Grades: PreK–2
- Level: Beginner
- Price: $0.99
- Tags: Projector, Streaming Media Player, Streaming Media Player, iPad, Android Tablet, General, Music Theory

- Description: Users listen to a selection of pitches sung by a group of adorable blobs. Students must listen to each blob and then listen to the king, then need to click the blob that matches pitch to the king. It works on a student's ability to match pitch and prepares them to listen to each other in an ensemble and tune together.

Google Expeditions
- Recommended Grades: 3–12
- Level: Beginner-Advanced
- Price: Based on product
- Tags: Projector, Streaming Media Player, iPad, Android Tablet, General, Cross-Curricular, Digital Field Trip
- Description: A virtual reality app created by Google, which has partnered with the likes of National Geographic and the American Museum of Natural History for this resource. Teachers can take groups of students on adventures through the Antarctic to discover about polar bears, fly to the Great Wall of China to learn more about the history of the country, or jump to the Amazon to observe chimpanzees. This is a tremendous cross-curricular tool that allows teachers to take students virtually out of the classroom. It can enable students to discover places in the world that they might not get a chance to visit otherwise.

Symphony Pro 5
- Recommended Grades: 7–12
- Level: Intermediate-Advanced
- Price: $14.99
- Tags: iPads, Streaming Media Player, General, Instrumental, Notation, Composing, Creating, Theory
- Description: This app is a great traditional notation software tool. With several editing capabilities, this app allows the user to draw directly into the program with a stylus or finger and arrange for any ensemble. This app makes it possible for students to compose anywhere, anytime.

Explain Everything
- Recommended Grades: K–4
- Level: Beginner-Intermediate
- Price: $14.99
- Tags: Mobile Device, Streaming Media Player, General, Creating, Composing, Assessment, Audio Recording
- Description: This app is used a lot in music education as an assessment tool for students to create a physical product to demonstrate their learning. Explain Everything is an interactive whiteboard app that lets students draw and record their voices. They can do activities such as writing out a rhythm and then record themselves while saying

the proper rhythm syllables. Students can also draw a brainstorming board about a specific topic with different facts about it, and record an oral presentation on the topic. Teachers can also use the app to record instruction to later share with students.

GarageBand
- Recommended Grades: 4–12
- Level: Beginner-Advanced
- Price: Free
- Tags: iPad, Streaming Media Player, General, Creating, Composing, Assessment, Audio Recording, Audio Editing
- Description: A powerful Apple-based audio editing software that is well known by almost all music educators. With interactive instruments, prebuilt loops of music, and recording and editing abilities, GarageBand is useful in many different ways. Students can create and edit podcasts, mix existing music, or record and create original stuff. They can also use just the interactive instruments to play together as a digital ensemble.

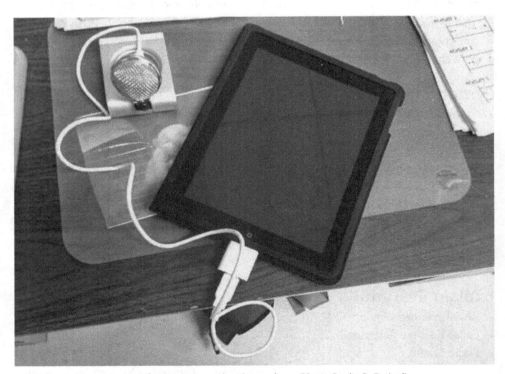

FIGURE 7.2 My quick setup for quick Garageband recordings (Photo Credit C. Dwinal)

Walk Band
- Recommended Grades: 4–12
- Level: Beginner-Advanced

- Price: Free
- Tags: Android Tablet, Chromebook, Streaming Media Player, General, Creating, Composing, Assessment, Audio Recording, Audio Editing
- Description: An Android-based audio recording and editing software that is an excellent alternative to Apple's GarageBand. With interactive instruments and audio recording and editing abilities, Walk Band is useful for a variety of different activities. Students can use digital instruments, mix existing music, or record and create original stuff.

Audio Evolution Mobile Studio
- Recommended Grades: 5–12
- Level: Beginner-Advanced
- Price: Free
- Tags: Android Tablet, Streaming Media Player, General, Creating, Composing, Assessment, Audio Recording, Audio Editing
- Description: Android-based audio editing software named an equivalent to Apple's GarageBand software. Users can use their Android tablets to do MIDI sequencing, play virtual instruments, and make playback loops.

iMovie
- Recommended Grades: 4–12
- Level: Beginner-Advanced
- Price: Free
- Tags: iPad, Streaming Media Player, Computer, Projector, General, Creating, Assessment, Video Recording, Video Editing
- Description: A powerful Apple-based video editing software for the computer or the iPad. Students can use the program to edit video footage and create top-notch videos and presentations. We use iMovie in my class to create. We make everything from music videos, commercials to discover more about some musical careers, and introductory videos on to how to play instruments.

FilmoraGo
- Recommended Grades: 5–12
- Level: Beginner-Advanced
- Price: Free
- Tags: Android Tablet, Streaming Media Player, General, Creating, Composing, Assessment, Video Recording, Video Editing
- Description: An Android-based video editing software named an equivalent to Apple's iMovie software. Users can use their Android tablets to do quick video editing, use pre-existing templates to bring videos to the next level, add music, make small enhancements to videos, and export final products to a variety of video platforms.

Book Creator

- Recommended Grades: 3–12
- Level: Beginner-Advanced
- Price: $4.99
- Tags: Projector, Streaming Media Player, iPad, Android Tablet, General, Creating, Literacy
- Description: This is a creative app that allows anyone to create an e-book that is perfect for immediate publishing. Can be used by multiple teachers in multiple subjects and can create a whole library of student-made books to access anytime that they want. All students can add pictures, videos, and design features to create an engaging story.

Stop Motion Studio

- Recommended Grades: 5–9
- Level: Intermediate-Advanced
- Price: Free
- Tags: Mobile Device, Streaming Media Player, General, Video Editing, Video Recording, Assessment
- Description: A video creation app that makes stop-motion animating easy. The user can make short easy videos right on the mobile device and compress it all into one final video. Perfect for students to create projects that show their knowledge about a subject they are learning in class. It can also be a motivator to have them go a little further beyond what they are already doing in classes.

Do Ink

- Recommended Grades: 2–10
- Level: Intermediate-Advanced
- Price: Based on product
- Tags: Projector, Interactive Board, General, Video Editing, Video Recording, Art Connection, Mobile Devices
- Description: A green screen and animation app that uses green screen technology to enhance videos that students make. This tool also has a library of animator tools for all users to improve their scenes with hand-drawn animations. Students can take projects they are making and go above and beyond what they could have made without a tool like this. Imagine students putting themselves in the middle of a disco dance club as they talk about 1970s music, or animating the life of Beethoven after they have done extensive research on the composer.

AR Makr

- Recommended Grades: 4–12
- Level: Intermediate-Advanced

- Price: Free
- Tags: Projector, Interactive Board, Augmented Reality, Virtual Reality, Creativity, Mobile Devices
- Description: An augmented reality creation platform that makes creating an AR experience easy for most ages. Users pick a flat surface then lay their drawings or photos into a space for a 3D experience.

Websites

Music Theory

- MusicTheory.net
- Recommended Grades: 9–12
- Level: Intermediate-Advanced
- Price: Based on product
- Tags: Projector, Interactive Board, General, Critical Thinking, Music Theory, Mobile Device
- Description: A more advanced music theory website with a large variety of drills that help older students practice theory, from essential to advanced levels. Students can also go through mini-lessons that cover everything from notes on a staff to chords in the second inversion. Perfect for small group work, extra credit, or to give a student a little extra help.

Interactive Instruments

- http://www.virtualmusicalinstruments.com
- Recommended Grades: 1–6
- Level: Beginner
- Price: Free
- Tags: Projector, Interactive Board, General, Instrumental, Playing, Ensembles, Modifications
- Description: A browser-based website with Flash instruments. The website has a unique selection of midi instruments that are interactive. The site also has a guitar tuner.

Interactive Whiteboard

- https://awwapp.com/#
- Recommended Grades: PreK–12
- Level: Beginner-Advanced
- Price: Free
- Tags: Projector, Interactive Board, General, Art Connection, Creating, Visual, Whiteboard

- Description: This is a cloud-based interactive whiteboard that is an alternative for teachers who might not have the opportunity to have a full physical interactive board at their fingertips. Teachers and students can write all over a blank board and then share and export it to save for later.

Padlet

- https://padlet.com
- Recommended Grades: 6–12
- Level: Beginner-Advanced
- Price: Free
- Tags: Projector, Interactive Board, General, Visual, Brainstorming, Collaboration
- Description: Teachers can set up spaces for students to comment and collaborate virtually for assignments and online coursework. Students can post ideas, research, or revelations and be able to comment on other student ideas and give feedback. Teachers can set up different boards to talk about various subjects, and they can export and share the work to protect student identities.

Popplet

- http://popplet.com
- Recommended Grades: 4–12
- Level: Beginner-Advanced
- Price: Free
- Tags: Projector, Interactive Board, General, Visual, Brainstorming, Collaboration
- Description: Popplet is a mind mapping tool that allows students and teachers to create mind maps easily and quickly to start planning and creating a visual for a new idea.

San Francisco Symphony Kids

- http://sfskids.org
- Recommended Grades: 2–5
- Level: Beginner-Intermediate
- Price: Free
- Tags: Projector, Interactive Board, General, Critical Thinking, Creating, Composing, Instruments, Listening and Analyzing, Mobile Devices, Flash
- Description: Students technically could use this program on any device as long as they have a Flash-based browser. Owned by the San Francisco Symphony, this website takes students on an adventure to learn more about classical music and the composers and instruments that create it. Students travel through various worlds to read fun facts and play games.

New York Philharmonic Kidzone

- http://www.nyphilkids.org
- Recommended Grades: 2–5

- Level: Beginner-Intermediate
- Price: Free
- Tags: Projector, Interactive Board, General, Critical Thinking, Creating, Composing, Instruments, Listening and Analyzing, Mobile Devices, Flash
- Description: Another Flash-based website, owned by the New York Philharmonic. It takes users backstage in the concert hall to play games about instruments and composers and then go onstage with the Philharmonic to experience music in an orchestra.

Classics for Kids

- ClassicsforKids.com
- Recommended Grades: PreK–5
- Level: Beginner
- Price: Free
- Tags: Projector, Interactive Board, General, Critical Thinking, Composers, Composing, Instruments, Listening and Analyzing, Mobile Devices
- Description: A website dedicated to music games and learning more about classical music and composers. Students can play basic music games, look up musical terms in the dictionary at their fingertips, and listen to a podcast on classical music. Teachers can get a plethora of lesson plans and activity sheets from this website to use in class!

Midnight Music

- MidnightMusic.com.au
- Recommended Grades: PreK–12
- Level: Beginner-Advanced
- Price: Based on product
- Tags: Projector, Interactive Board, General, Ensemble, Teacher Resources, Critical Thinking, Creating, Composing, Music Theory
- Description: A fantastic website of teacher resources integrating technology into teaching music created by the brilliant Katie Wardrobe. This resource has lesson suggestions, resource ideas, and teacher training for all educators. Katie also has an extensive library of training videos, a regular podcast, and a resource guide that she publishes every year. She also has some very cool resources for how to integrate film scoring into lessons.

Teoría

- Teoria.com
- Recommended Grades: 9–12
- Level: Intermediate-Advanced
- Price: Free
- Tags: Projector, Interactive Board, General, Critical Thinking, Music Theory, Mobile Device

- Description: Similar to MusicTheory.net, Teoria provides intermediate to advanced exercises and lessons covering multiple music theory topics from intervals to key signatures to scales. Students can also go through short lessons about specific topics.

Soundtrap

- Soundtrap.com
- Recommended Grades: 6–12
- Level: Intermediate-Advanced
- Price: Based on product
- Tags: Projector, Interactive Board, General, Critical Thinking, Creating, Composing, Mobile Devices, Collaboration
- Description: Cloud-based composing software. Students can collaborate in real time on any device in any part of the world to record, mix, use loops, and more to create music. Teachers can use Soundtrap for Education to assign lessons and assignments and give students plenty of opportunities to collaborate. The program can integrate into well known learning management systems.

Soundation

- Soundation.com
- Recommended Grades: 8–12
- Level: Intermediate-Advanced
- Price: Based on product
- Tags: Projector, Interactive Board, General, Critical Thinking, Creating, Composing, Mobile Devices, Collaboration
- Description: Cloud-based composing and sharing software. Users can record, mix, add hundreds of loops and effects, and then share on a platform similar to Soundcloud. This resource has excellent free accounts, but once a user purchases a reasonably priced pro account, it unlocks more tools that allow them to go beyond just the basics. One warning: There are many beginning artists on the platform who are sharing their uncensored, explicit music and lyrics.

MuseScore

- Musescore.org
- Recommended Grades: 4–12
- Level: Beginner-Advanced
- Price: Free
- Tags: Projector, Interactive Board, General, Critical Thinking, Creating, Composing, Desktops, Laptops, Notation
- Description: A free composition and notation software that is open-source and midi-capable. Anyone can download this software to use on their device. Users have access

to over 5,000 scores in the program as a jumping-off point. They then can share their creations with other like-minded composers and get feedback on their work.

Chrome Music Lab
- https://musiclab.chromeexperiments.com
- Recommended Grades: PreK–7
- Level: Beginner-Advanced
- Price: Based on product
- Tags: Projector, Interactive Board, General, Critical Thinking, Creating
- Description: An innovative set of music creation tools that allow students to create and make music at many different levels. They have a variety of various synthesizers and drum machines to move shapes and pictures around to experiment with different sounds, tempos, and rhythms. This set of tools also has excellent connections to the science of sound and how your ear hears the music discussions or activities.

Music Tech Teacher
- MusicTechTeacher.com
- Recommended Grades: 3–12
- Level: Beginner-Intermediate
- Price: Free
- Tags: Projector, Interactive Board, General, Critical Thinking, Creating, Composing, Games, Teacher Resources
- Description: A comprehensive resource by Karen Garrett that includes quizzes, lessons, worksheets, and games. The quizzes are Flash-based games that are great practice and drill activities. Many of the experiences are based around the music technology lab but have many other uses.

Audio Recorder
- Vocaroo.com
- Recommended Grades: 6–12
- Level: Intermediate
- Price: Free
- Tags: General, Critical Thinking, Creating, Composing, Audio Recording, Laptop, Desktop
- Description: A cloud-based audio recording tool. Users can hit the record button, use the built-in mic in their computer, and then export as a separate file to share or email assignments and assessments!

Jeopardy Labs
- JeopardyLabs.com
- Recommended Grades: 5–12

- Level: Beginner-Advanced
- Price: Free accounts and $20 for a lifetime VIP membership
- Tags: Projector, Interactive Board, General, Critical Thinking, Assessment, Games, Practice
- Description: An easy way to create a Jeopardy-style game with an already built template. Input your questions and get a beautiful game ready to play, no extra programming needed. You will need to pay extra to be able to embed audio and video media and link them to questions. This tool is excellent, especially for a whole group assessment or a check for comprehension activity at the end of a unit. You can build a variety of different ones and have students compete against each other as a review. Divide up into teams and ask students to answer the questions in groups to see who can come out as Jeopardy winners.

SafeShare

- SafeShare.TV
- Recommended Grades: PreK–12
- Level: Beginner-Intermediate
- Price: Free plans or $4.99/Month for Premium
- Tags: Projector, Interactive Board, General, Video Editing, YouTube, Security, Internet Filters, Teacher Resources, Utilities
- Description: SafeShare is for those who are sick of having to deal with the ads on YouTube and other video sites. The website filters out all of the malicious ads and unfriendly spam from Internet videos and makes them classroom-friendly.

QR Code Creator

- QRStuff.com
- Recommended Grades: 2–12
- Level: Beginner-Advanced
- Price: Based on product
- Tags: Projector, Interactive Board, General, Instrumental, Choral, Teacher Resources, Utilities
- Description: QRStuff is a QR code maker that can make QR Codes in a snap. All you need to do is input the URL you would want students to go to and export the code. With this tool, teachers can create a QR code with anything from a YouTube video, to a website URL, to a PDF file. These QR codes last forever and work with any QR code reader. This tool is excellent for creating a link to your weekly practice sheets to connecting sheet music and MP3 recordings of music for an upcoming concert for students to take home to practice.

Kahoot

- Kahoot.com
- Recommended Grades: 4–12

- Level: Beginner-Advanced
- Price: Free accounts, $1/month for Pro, $3/month for Pro
- Tags: Projector, Interactive Board, General, Critical Thinking, Assessment, Games, Competition
- Description: Kahoot is a tool that allows teachers to create assessment games that can be taken individually or in teams using any smart-enabled device. Students can go to Kahoot.it, input a game PIN, and be taken directly to their game. They then can answer questions directly from their smart device. It will give them a certain number of points based on accuracy and speed. Students can compare scores, and a winner comes out in the end. Teachers can use premade templates, or they can create their own!

ClassDojo

- https://www.classdojo.com
- Recommended Grades: PreK–12
- Level: Beginner-Advanced
- Price: Based on product
- Tags: Projector, Interactive Board, General, Instrumental, Choral, Teacher Resources, Utilities, Classroom Management
- Description: ClassDojo is a classroom management tool used by teachers and schools all over the world. Students can earn points for behavior that meets or goes beyond classroom expectations; or can get points taken away. Teachers can also take notes on a child's behavior, notify parents of anything that is happening, and award excellent behavior and incredible milestones that students achieve. A lot of teachers use it as a marketplace award system where students can cash in points for special privileges. It is a tool that can be used in several classes throughout a student's day.

CoSpaces Edu

- https://cospaces.io/edu/
- Recommended Grades: 4–12
- Level: Beginner-Advanced
- Price: Based on product
- Tags: Projector, Interactive Board, General, Critical Thinking, Creating, Virtual Reality, Project-Based Learning, Mobile Devices
- Description: CoSpaces Edu is a virtual reality creator that students can experiment with. Teachers can use it as a way to create interactive experiences for students to use with an interactive board or virtual reality viewer. Have students travel through the world to experience the learning rather than see it on a 2D surface. Students can use it to create final projects that demonstrate their learning. They can bring orchestras to life to demonstrate knowledge of instruments at the end of a unit. Students can also see a group of Native performers in their traditional outfits while stating facts about their music and culture. Projects are then inserted into VR viewers for an immersive experience.

Skype in the Classroom

- https://education.skype.com/

Recommended Grades: 2–12

- Level: Beginner-Advanced
- Price: Free
- Tags: Projector, Interactive Board, Band, General, Choral
- Description: A place to collaborate with other educators to learn about connecting classrooms from opposite sides of the world. Schedule Skype times with other teachers and get tips and tricks on video conferencing in the classroom. Skyping allows you to break down the four walls of the traditional classroom and show students a world beyond, that they might not otherwise experience.

Instrument Safari

- http://listeningadventures.carnegiehall.org
- Recommended Grades: K–3
- Level: Intermediate-Advanced
- Price: Free
- Tags: Interactive Board, General, Critical Thinking, Outdoor Adventure
- Description: Using Benjamin Britten's *Young Person's Guide to the Orchestra*, this site takes you through an adventure to collect all of the missing instruments. Uncle Ollie asks you and his niece, Violet, to obtain the missing instruments and bring them back to the stage to perform as an ensemble once again. This site is high-energy and keeps students engaged for hours.

ViewPure.com

- Recommended Grades: PreK–12
- Level: Beginner-Advanced
- Price: Based on product
- Tags: Projector, Interactive Board, General, Video Editing, YouTube, Security, Internet Filters, Teacher, Utilities
- Description: Similar to SafeShareTV, ViewPure filters out the comments, ads, and suggested videos from online video platforms. A great tool to use when showing YouTube videos to the younger students because you can prevent those ugly comments and ads that make you dash to the whiteboard to skip ahead.

Incredibox

- https://www.incredibox.com
- Recommended Grades: 2–8
- Level: Beginner-Advanced
- Price: Free

- Tags: Interactive Board, General, Critical Thinking, Creating, Beatboxing, Ostinatos
- Description: An excellent looping tool to teach kids about vocal ostinatos and relating it to current hip-hop and rap music. Drag loops onto the ensemble to create and record your masterpiece. Have students make accompaniment tracks for raps, learn how to perform together, and more.

Quaver's Marvelous World of Music
- https://www.quavermusic.com
- Recommended Grades: PreK–8
- Level: Beginner-Advanced
- Price: Varies based on product
- Tags: Projector, Interactive Board, General, Critical Thinking, Creating, Composing, Curriculum
- Description: Quaver is a cloud-based, customizable, PreK–8 library of searchable digital curriculum and resources. Quaver includes a full curriculum plus song-based and topic-based materials able to be customized for any teaching style. It works on just about any device and makes learning seriously fun for all of your students and you as the teacher.

Drum Machine
- Drumbit.app
- Recommended Grades: 1–12
- Level: Beginner-Advanced
- Price: Free
- Tags: Projector, General, Critical Thinking, Creating, Digital Instrument, Ostinatos, Bucket Drumming, Rhythm Sticks
- Description: A web-based drum machine that brings the comforts of professional-grade equipment to your device. Use the software to break down different rhythms and create and compose music. All students can share with friends and connect this app with careers in the music field.

Scratch Coding
- https://scratch.mit.edu
- Recommended Grades: 2–12
- Level: Advanced
- Price: Free
- Tags: Interactive Board, Streaming Media Player, General, Critical Thinking, Creating, Composing, Coding
- Description: Scratch is a simple programming platform meant to teach kids the basics of coding. Scratch is a perfect way to show students that someone like them can create all of those digital instruments they see online.

Dallas Symphony Orchestra for Kids

- https://www.mydso.com/dso-kids/
- Recommended Grades: PreK–3
- Level: Beginner
- Price: Free
- Tags: Projector, Interactive Board, General, Critical Thinking, Listening, Instruments, Orchestra
- Description: A resource site developed by the Dallas Symphony Orchestra with great listening examples and activity suggestions. And if you are around Dallas, you can look into scheduling a visit!

Isle of Tune

- http://isleoftune.com
- Recommended Grades: K–3
- Level: Beginner-Intermediate
- Price: Free
- Tags: Interactive Board, General, Critical Thinking, Listening, Creating, Composing, Cross-Curricular
- Description: This website is a music creation tool that allows your students to build their musical community. Every rock, sign, house, even stoplight has its own sound when the cars drive past.

Noteflight

- https://www.noteflight.com
- Recommended Grades: 3–12
- Level: Beginner-Advanced
- Price: Based on product
- Tags: Projector, Interactive Board, General, Critical Thinking, Creating, Composing
- Description: This program is a high-powered compositional tool. With the ability to bring up the cloud-based creation tool on any device, the possibilities for composing at every grade level are endless.

SoundCloud

- https://soundcloud.com
- Recommended Grades: 4–12
- Level: Intermediate-Advanced
- Price: Free
- Tags: Projector, Interactive Board, General, Creating, Composing, Music Production

Description: A simple song-sharing system where you can upload originals, create playlists, and generate unique links to share work. A great place if you like to create your own work and use it in lessons. One of my favorite uses is to create podcasts and bring them up during class to listen to.

Bouncy Ball Noise Meter

- https://bouncyballs.org
- Recommended Grades: PreK–5
- Level: Beginner-Advanced
- Price: Free
- Tags: Projector, Interactive Board, General, Choral, Band, Classroom Management, Choral, Dynamics
- Description: A simple noise meter which starts to go crazy if the decibels in the room get over a certain level. Perfect for taming a louder classroom, or even to work on the dynamics of a piece of music.

Edpuzzle

- https://edpuzzle.com
- Recommended Grades: 4–12
- Level: Beginner-Advanced
- Price: Free for all
- Tags: Projector, Streaming Media Player, General, Utilities, Mobile Devices, Laptop, Desktop, Assessment, Teacher Resources
- Description: A content resource that allows teachers to assign short video lessons to their students through either the site itself or as upload through Google Classroom. You can also upload your lessons too, and use materials from other content creation services such as YouTube and Khan Academy.

Flipgrid

- https://flipgrid.com
- Recommended Grades: 3–12
- Level: Beginner-Advanced
- Price: Free for all
- Tags: Projector, Streaming Media Player, General, Utilities, Mobile Devices, Laptop, Desktop, Assessment, Video Recording
- Description: A video assessment resource that allows students to record their answers and to send them to teachers for review and grading. Teachers can create little lessons with discussion starters, and students can respond via video from any device. This tool can be useful for asynchronous learning, flipped classroom models, and even small group or individual 1:1 activities inside of class.

Nearpod

- https://nearpod.com
- Recommended Grades: 2–12
- Level: Beginner-Advanced
- Price: Based on Product
- Tags: Projector, Streaming Media Player, General, Utilities, Mobile Devices, Laptop, Desktop, Assessment, Teacher Resources
- Description: A perfect tool for personalized learning using 1:1 devices. Teachers can find or create lessons within their account and then assign them to students to complete and assess right inside of the resource. Students and teachers can access the resources from anywhere on any device, including smartphones!

Groovy Music

- https://www.musicfirst.com/applications/groovy-music/
- Recommended Grades: PreK–2
- Level: Beginner
- Price: Based on product
- Tags: Projector, Interactive Board, General, Creating, Composing
- Description: Groovy Music is a general music sequencer with different themes built for younger students to compose and create. They can drag shapes and different pictures on the board to create different melodies and rhythms. Students can also overlay their creations on a staff to start making the connection between the visual manipulatives they have been using and where they belong on the staff.

JoyTunes Recorder

- https://www.joytunes.com/game.php
- Recommended Grades: 3–12
- Level: Beginner-Intermediate
- Price: Based on product
- Tags: Mobile Device, Streaming Media Player, General, Instrumental, Playing, Ensembles, Recorder, Flash, Projector, Computer
- Description: This program is controlled by what students play on their recorders. A lot of the games in the app are focused on breath support, matching pitch, and playing notes on target. Students must make sure to keep the cat flying the plane and keep away the birds from messing up the targets!

Audacity

- https://www.audacityteam.org/download/
- Recommended Grades: 6–12
- Level: Intermediate-Advanced

- Price: Free
- Tags: Projector, Interactive Board, General, Creating, Composing, Music Production, Audio Editing, Audio Recording
- Description: A tried and true audio editing software used by many audio editing enthusiasts, students, and music educators. With Audacity, it makes it easier to take tracks you want to have students sing with and edit them the way you like. I often edit instrumental tracks for performances and put them in a playlist for the show. Sometimes I need to take out the vocals, slow things down, or add in a quiet bass drum tap to help the singers keep the beat.

StaffWars

- http://www.themusicinteractive.com/downloads.html
- Recommended Grades: 3–10
- Level: Beginner-Intermediate
- Price: Based on product
- Tags: Projector, Interactive Board, General, Ensemble, Music Theory, Mobile Devices, Streaming Media Player
- Description: This software has both desktop and mobile versions which allow for gameplay on any device. Users watch notes come on a staff on the screen and must choose the correct answer to see the spaceship blast the note apart. In the live version, they must play the right note on their instrument to get the same result. Recommended for up to grade 10, but I have had undergraduate college students that were very engaged with it! It is a fun and engaging way for students to practice learning how to read music.

YouTube

- YouTube.com
- Recommended Grades: K–12
- Level: Beginner-Advanced
- Price: Free
- Tags: Mobile Device, Streaming Media Player, General, Visuals, Videos, Projector, Computer
- Description: A platform for sharing videos about pretty much anything. It can turn into a private place to upload your performance videos and save videos you would like to share with your students. You will need to be careful of the content in this site; the best course of action is to usually curate playlists of the videos you would like to show students before class.

Drawing Tool

- YouiDraw.com
- Recommended Grades: PreK–12

- Level: Intermediate-Advanced
- Price: Free
- Tags: Projector, Interactive Board, General, Art Connection, Creating, Visual
- Description: A free and simpler version of Photoshop. This software provides a large variety of templates to choose from, or you can start from a blank slate and go from there. An excellent alternative to those who do not have an interactive board or inter-activity on their board. You can save work later to show off student learning.

SMART Notebook Software

- https://education.smarttech.com/products/notebook
- Recommended Grades: PreK–12
- Level: Beginner-Advanced
- Price: Based on product
- Tags: Projector, SMART Board, General, Critical Thinking, Creating, Composing, Utilities
- Description: Software specifically meant for the SMART interactive board line. Using this software, teachers can create interactive activities to use during classes. Imagine teachers creating a staff and manipulatives themselves and being able to have students compose and create using different visuals. They could also have older students build interactive boards about musical styles or composers. There are uses at both ends of the age spectrum.

Finale Notepad Software

- https://www.finalemusic.com/products/notepad/
- Recommended Grades: 3–12
- Level: Beginner-Advanced
- Price: Free (Just for this specific product; all other Finale products require purchase)
- Tags: Projector, Interactive Board, General, Critical Thinking, Creating, Composing, Desktops, Laptops, Notation
- Description: An old favorite when it comes to composing software that many music educators use daily. Can be used in a computer class setting or as a full group. Educators can input music into this composition and notation software for lesson resources, compose on the spot with students, or have students create their works of art.

ActivInspire

- https://support.prometheanworld.com/product/activinspire
- Recommended Grades: PreK–12
- Level: Beginner-Advanced
- Price: Based on product
- Tags: Projector, Interactive Board, General, Critical Thinking, Creating, Composing, Utilities

- Description: This is the Promethean board version of the SMART Notebook software. Use this software to bring up blank screens when you are brainstorming ideas and notate what is on your screen as you have discussions with your students during the lessons.

Buncee

- https://app.edu.buncee.com/schools
- Recommended Grades: PreK–12
- Level: Beginner-Advanced
- Price: Based on product
- Tags: Projector, Interactive Board, General Music, Critical Thinking, Creating, Personalized Learning, Assessments, Collaboration
- Description: This is a perfect tool to integrate more personalized learning into your instruction. Create lesson visuals, build collaborative spaces, and even create assessments for students. This tool is ideal for a 1:1 student-to-device environment.

8

Conclusion

My projector and computer are the heart of my classroom. Even though I don't use them every day, they are something we still gather around at the beginning of every class. They have become "part of the family" without me even realizing it. When I reflect on why it became that way, I think it was because they were the first two pieces of technology I had in my room, and they are what I use the most.

It all started with finding the right reasons to use them. During my first year of teaching, I needed to look at the lessons I was writing and see where I could make them better. If I were giving a lecture on rock 'n' roll music, for example, it would be even better if it included pictures and video of the people and things that I was talking about.

There was one time I wanted my choirs to do a show with all Beatles music. I tried my hardest to describe the band to them during rehearsals, but students finally understood what the Beatles were all about after seeing pictures and films of them in concert. The projector helped me share those things with them.

There are times when younger students need more practice learning how to read notes on the staff, and even though flashcards and composing on paper are fine for a little while, activities like Quaver's Staff Champion games or StaffWars add something special. We can do them together using the projector. The simple activities take on new meaning when there is a little bit of technology added. It is not something we use all the time, but after spending a few weeks getting introduced to music theory and other concepts taught in music class, students have the chance to apply their learned knowledge when they are given different avenues of gameplay.

We also use the systems as a group. It is a way of bringing the class together to work toward a common goal, whether they are having a good day or a bad day. The projector has become a common gathering area, rather than just a piece of technology.

Interactive Visual Ideas for Musical Classroom Activities. Catherine Dwinal, Oxford University Press (2020). © Oxford University Press.
DOI: 10.1093/oso/9780190929855.001.0001

FIGURE 8.1 Students egaged in a video chat with a class from across the country (Photo Credit C. Dwinal)

With the power of social media and networking, it is easier to connect with teachers across the globe to learn more when it comes to interactive projection systems. I jump on Twitter and involve myself in chats with all kinds of other music educators; you can too. I also use other platforms like Facebook and join groups like the large Music Teachers group, to chat with even more teachers from across the globe and get more ideas. With social media, I am no longer stuck on an island away from my colleagues.

After being in my classroom for a while, I have the motivation to show music educators everywhere that the key to success is not what you have, but how you use it. An interactive display might be helpful for your classroom, but if you use it only as a TV, you need some assistance to use it to its full potential. There are simple yet effective ways to use the interactive display beyond using it as just a display screen.

I was in my second year of teaching. I had just come back from a mind-blowing conference and just happened to be attending the district technology committee meeting. As we were getting ready for the meeting, I struck up a conversation with our IT director about streaming media players.

They were brand new and had just come onto the market. I had had a long conversation with a friend at the conference about how to incorporate them into music class instruction. I shared the conversation with our IT director. He was so impressed that I had a brand new streaming media player sitting on my desk the very next week.

The lesson here is that if you know you are ready to use a new piece of technology, and you do not have it, it never hurts to ask. The key to incorporating technology-based resources into the music classroom is, first, to get the right equipment in the room. Sometimes it is just a matter of proving to the administration that you would use it.

Money is always a factor when acquiring technology resources. If you hear a "no," it is never the end of the road. Change your "that's the end of that" mentality to "let's try something else." Instead, look for a discount site to see if you can get the same equipment for cheaper, or try to find used or refurbished equipment from another place. You do not need to have brand new equipment in your room to get the most out of it and use it in creative and inventive ways in your classroom.

Grants and fundraising are other routes to take. Check your state department of education website for technology grants that you can apply for. For things like this, you will need to make sure that you have a project to do for these grants if you get selected. How can you create a project for an application like this? It's not about suggesting, "That would be cool to have!" It is about finding a specific need for the tool first. It could answer an essential question like "Can studying music assist in early childhood brain development?"

FIGURE 8.2 Composing their next masterpieces on their netbooks (Photo Credit C. Dwinal)

Come up with a robust topic and accurate data when advocating for your program, and prove why music overall is essential. Reflect on what you do every day; do you have a problem to solve, or something that could be better if you had a tool to help you? For example, do you run into the problem of having to assess your students all in person and in one class? Do you want iPads in the room for recording assessments? What about a working projection system for projecting visuals for class?

When looking for a grant, try to get the best technology you can. If you are unsure where to start, your district might have a grant writer already on staff you can speak with. You could also talk with your principal. Make sure to connect with your IT department as well; they will be the ones to help you get your equipment up and running and will help maintain it.

In my second year of teaching, I worked with our physical education teacher on a grant project. She was already well versed in grant writing and a very brilliant educator. We caught wind of a technology grant becoming available in the following weeks and pulled a project together that related the steady beat of the music to a heartbeat.

Students learned about their heartbeat in PE and took their pulse at three different physical exercise paces. They then took those speeds into music class, where we used them as tempos for a piece of music they were writing. Through the grant for this project, we gained several iPod Touches and a few iPads that we were able to use in our instruction. It was a great experience that allowed my colleague and me to acquire more technology, which we used for our instruction for a long time.

One last way to gain funding for the projection system you want is to reach out to a local business that could sponsor your classroom. You might have a local law office or even a community pizza joint that would love to help you get the tools you need to teach.

Using new technology can seem overwhelming at first. It is easier if you start by using it in class a little at a time. Scientifically, our human brains can only absorb so much information at one time. To be able to master a skill, you need to pace yourself and be ready to learn it in small chunks, just like you would teach it to a student.

Think of it like you are coming back from a workshop or conference. First, take all the information you have been collecting about your technology and divide it into lists by type of devices you have available. Next, focus on each list and figure out if there are any similarities in the information presented, to categorize them in more detail.

Look through each piece of information you have and find at least two new activities or resources that you could try tomorrow with your classes. Then find two new things that you could do a couple of months from now. Then find one new thing that you do not think you will ever be able to do, but it would be great if you could.

Do this for each list you have until you have five activities for each tool. Then set goals for what you want to do with the new tools you have discovered. Keep those close, especially when you are lesson planning.

The activities from your lists that you could do tomorrow would be easy to fit into your existing lessons. After you try one the first time, reflect on how it went and what you could do better, then try it again. How did the next time go? Next time you use it, make it your own and start to augment those activities into something a little bit different and more customized to your instructional needs.

Activities that you picked out to possibly do a few months from now could be integrated into a future unit plan, as a bigger goal. This would give you a long time to think about what you want to do. You could take your time to research, practice, and prepare as you are getting comfortable with the technology through other simpler activities. When it comes time for the unit or lesson, you can plan it out with a colleague or technology coach who can help you. After you feel more comfortable with the technology and have stepped just slightly out of your comfort zone, direct your attention to that larger goal. Ask yourself the question, "How can my current instruction be tailored toward reaching the larger goal?" This goal will take some time to achieve, but it will be very satisfying for you, and worthwhile for your students.

There are a lot of activities and projects in this publication that you can use as larger goals, and a lot of activities you can do right now. Take a look at one of the more significant projects and pick that as your biggest goal. Use the simple activities that are labeled for beginners as great I-Can-Do-This-Tomorrows in the section titled as such, found at

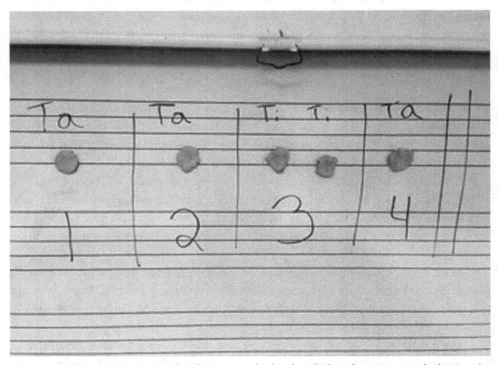

FIGURE 8.3 Sometimes we just need to throw some playdough at the board to compose a rhythm in order to start class (Photo Credit C. Dwinal)

the beginning of the book. Start easy, start simple, then move to the more significant projects and your larger goal.

The content in this book is plentiful and organized by device, grade, and level of difficulty. Think of each chapter as a bank of ideas for you to be able to pick what is going to work for you.

The sky's the limit when you are trying something new. Always remember, though, start small and build. Feel comfortable with your activities and instruction before moving on to the next thing, and always know that it is perfectly fine to change your plan and leave it out if you don't yet feel comfortable with it. Use technology meaningfully in your teaching and see how powerful it can be!

Activities Categorized by Device Type

Find each activity labeled by grade level and learning activity type.

Projectors

Websites with Visual Material (PreK–12, Appreciating)
Brainstorming Activities (PreK–12, Connecting)
Background Projection (PreK–12, Performing)
Noise Meter (K–5, Listening, Connecting)
Audience Sing-Along (K–9, Appreciating, Listening, Performing)
Watching YouTube Clips (K–12, Listening, Connecting)
Introduction to the Drum Set (1–4, Composing)
Composing (2–7, Composing)
Movement Break (2–8, Moving)
Concert Performance Video Playback (2–12, Listening, Appreciating)
Skype (2–12, Connecting, Performing)
Projecting Music to Play (2–12, Performing)
Webquests (2–12, Creating, Connecting)
Animation Clips (3–12, Composing, Creating, Connecting)
Green Screen Movie Project (4–12, Composing, Creating, Connecting)
Make Your Own Projector (5–9, Creating, Connecting)
Story Movie (5–12, Composing, Creating, Connecting)
Found Sounds (6–12, Composing, Creating)
Guitar Sheet Music (6–12, Composing, Performing)

Interactive Boards and TVs

Visual Scores (PreK–7, Listening, Appreciating)
Make Your Own SMART Board Activities (PreK–8, Connecting)
Interactive Morning Message (PreK–12, Connecting)
Instrument Safari (K–2, Listening, Appreciating, Connecting)

Musical Community Activity (K–3, Composing, Creating, Listening, Connecting)

Interactive Games (K–7, Connecting)

How Does This Music Feel Activity (1–6, Listening, Appreciating, Connecting)

Incredibox (2–6, Composing, Listening, Performing)

Projecting Music to Play and Notate (2–12, Performing)

Centers (3–7, Composing, Creating, Connecting)

Interactive Storytelling (3–10, Composing, Listening, Connecting)

Creating Accompaniment Tracks (3–12, Composing)

Composing Pieces on Noteflight (3–12, Composing)

Create Your Story Music (3–12, Composing, Creating, Listening)

Composer Research (4–12, Creating, Appreciating, Connecting)

Exit Tickets (4–12, Connecting)

World Music Presentation (7–11, Creating, Appreciating, Connecting)

Audio Engineering (7–12, Composing, Connecting)

Document Cameras

High-Low, Loud-Soft Shadow Movements (PreK–1, Listening, Moving)

Quick Instruction Visuals (PreK–5, Connecting)

Hack Attack: Hacking Your Document Camera for Video Chatting and Pictures (PreK–12, Connecting, Performing)

Manipulatives (K–3, Composing, Creating)

Note Identify Flashcard Game (K–3, Connecting)

Puppet Show (1–3, Creating, Connecting)

Notating a Piece of Music (5–12, Performing)

Drawing Storyboards (6–8, Creating, Connecting)

Ensemble Practice Instruction (6–12, Performing)

Streaming Media Players

Remote Desktop Activities (PreK–12, Connecting)

Interactive Instruments (PreK–12, Performing)

Explain Everything (K–6, Composing)

Metaverse Assessments and Word Hunt (K–8, Creating, Moving, Connecting)

Recording and Showing Performances and Informances (K–12, Listening, Performing)

GarageBand Activities (3–6, Composing, Creating)

Recorder Games (3–6, Listening, Performing)

MadPad (3–7, Composing, Creating, Performing)

StaffWars (4–12, Connecting)

Drum Machine Accompaniment (4–12, Composing, Creating, Performing)

News Crew (5–12, Creating, Appreciating, Connecting)
Virtual Field Trip (6–12, Creating, Appreciating, Connecting)
History of Rock 'n' Roll (8–12, Creating, Appreciating, Connecting

Activities by Difficulty

Find each activity categorized by difficulty level

Beginner

Websites with Visual Material
Background Projection
Noise Meter
Brainstorming Activities
Watching YouTube Clips
Concert Performance Video Playback
Movement Break
Projecting Music to Play
Interactive Morning Message
Interactive Games
How Does This Music Feel Activity
Incredibox
Projecting Music to Play and Notate
Composing Pieces on Noteflight
Exit Tickets
High-Low, Loud-Soft Shadow Movements
Quick Instruction Visuals
Manipulatives
Note Identify Flashcard Game
Puppet Show
Notating a Piece of Music
Ensemble Practice Instruction
Recording and Showing Performances and Informances
StaffWars
Interactive Instruments

Moderate

Audience Sing-Along
Introduction to the Drum Set
Composing

Skype
Make Your Own Projector
Found Sounds
Guitar Sheet Music
Visual Scores
Make Your Own SMART Board Activities
Musical Community Activity
Centers
Creating Accompaniment Tracks
Create Your Own Story Music
Composer Research
Hack Attack: Hacking Your Document Camera for Video Chatting and Pictures
Drawing Storyboards
Explain Everything
GarageBand Activities
Drum Machine Accompaniment
Recorder Games
MadPad

Expert

Webquests
Animation Clips
Green Screen Movie Project
Story Movie
Instrument Safari
Interactive Storytelling
World Music Presentation
Audio Engineering
Metaverse Assessments and Word Hunt
News Crew
Virtual Field Trip
History of Rock 'n' Roll

Activities Categorized by Grade Range

Find each activity categorized by recommended grade range and labeled with those that include the use of student personal devices.

Extra Mobile Devices Recommended = *

Pre-Kindergarten through Second Grade

- Noise Meter
- Watching YouTube Clips
- Concert Performance Video Playback
- Websites with Visual Material
- Brainstorming Activities
- Composing
- Introduction to the Drum Set
- Skype
- Background Projection
- Audience Sing-Along
- Projecting Music to Play
- Movement Break
- Webquests*
- Make Your Own SMART Board Activities
- Interactive Morning Message
- Instrument Safari*
- Interactive Games
- Visual Scores
- Projecting Music to Play and Notate
- Incredibox*
- Musical Community Activity*
- How Does This Music Feel Activity
- Puppet Show*
- High-Low, Loud-Soft Shadow Movements
- Manipulatives
- Quick Instruction Visuals
- Note Identify Flashcard Game
- Hack Attack: Hacking Your Document Camera for Video Chatting and Pictures
- Explain Everything*
- Recording and Showing Performances and Informances
- Remote Desktop Activities
- Metaverse Assessments and Word Hunt*
- Interactive Instruments*

Third Grade through Fifth Grade

- Noise Meter
- Watching YouTube Clips
- Concert Performance Video Playback
- Websites with Visual Material

- Brainstorming Activities
- Composing
- Introduction to the Drum Set
- Skype
- Background Projection
- Green Screen Movie Project*
- Audience Sing-Along
- Projecting Music to Play
- Make Your Own Projector*
- Movement Break
- Story Movie*
- Animation Clips*
- Webquests*
- Make Your Own SMART Board Activities
- Interactive Morning Message
- Creating Accompaniment Tracks*
- Composing Pieces on Noteflight*
- Interactive Games*
- Centers*
- Composer Research*
- Visual Scores*
- Interactive Storytelling*
- Projecting Music to Play and Notate
- Incredibox*
- Musical Community Activity*
- Create Your Own Story Music*
- How Does This Music Feel Activity
- Exit Tickets
- Puppet Show*
- Manipulatives
- Quick Instruction Visuals
- Notating a Piece of Music
- Note Identify Flashcard Game
- Hack Attack: Hacking Your Document Camera for Video Chatting and Pictures
- GarageBand Activities*
- StaffWars*
- Explain Everything*
- Recording and Showing Performances and Informances
- Drum Machine Accompaniment*
- Remote Desktop Activities
- Metaverse Assessments and Word Hunt*

- Interactive Instruments*
- Recorder Games*
- MadPad*

Sixth Grade through Eighth Grade
- Watching YouTube Clips
- Concert Performance Video Playback
- Websites with Visual Material
- Composing
- Skype
- Background Projection
- Green Screen Movie Project*
- Audience Sing-Along
- Projecting Music to Play
- Make Your Own Projector*
- Movement Break
- Story Movie*
- Animation Clips*
- Found Sounds*
- Guitar Sheet Music*
- Webquests*
- Make Your Own SMART Board Activities
- Interactive Morning Message
- Creating Accompaniment Tracks*
- Composing Pieces on Noteflight*
- Interactive Games
- Centers*
- Composer Research*
- Visual Scores
- Interactive Storytelling*
- Projecting Music to Play and Notate
- Incredibox*
- Create Your Own Story Music*
- How Does This Music Feel Activity
- World Music Presentation*
- Exit Tickets
- Drawing Storyboards*
- Ensemble Practice Instruction
- Notating a Piece of Music
- Hack Attack: Hacking Your Document Camera for Video Chatting and Pictures
- StaffWars*

- GarageBand Activities*
- Explain Everything*
- Recording and Showing Performances and Informances
- Drum Machine Accompaniment*
- Remote Desktop Activities
- Metaverse Assessments and Word Hunt*
- Interactive Instruments*
- Recorder Games*
- MadPad*
- Virtual Field Trip*
- History of Rock 'n' Roll*
- News Crew*

Ninth Grade through Twelfth Grade

- Watching YouTube Clips
- Concert Performance Video Playback
- Websites with Visual Material
- Brainstorming Activities
- Skype
- Background Projection
- Green Screen Movie Project*
- Audience Sing-Along
- Projecting Music to Play
- Make Your Own Projector*
- Story Movie*
- Animation Clips*
- Found Sounds*
- Guitar Sheet Music*
- Webquests*
- Interactive Morning Message
- Creating Accompaniment Tracks*
- Composing Pieces on Noteflight*
- Interactive Storytelling*
- Projecting Music to Play and Notate
- Create Your Own Story Music*
- World Music Presentation*
- Exit Tickets
- Ensemble Practice Instruction
- Notating a Piece of Music
- Hack Attack: Hacking Your Document Camera for Video Chatting and Pictures

- StaffWars*
- Recording and Showing Performances and Informances
- Drum Machine Accompaniment*
- Remote Desktop Activities
- Interactive Instruments*
- Virtual Field Trip*
- History of Rock 'n' Roll*
- News Crew*

Bibliography

Puentedura, R. (2014, December 11). "SAMR and TPCK: A Hands-On Approach to Classroom Practice." Retrieved from http://www.hippasus.com/rrpweblog/archives/2014_12.html

Moses, L. (2014, March 11). "A Look at Kids' Exposure to Ads." Retrieved from https://www.adweek.com/digital/look-kids-exposure-ads-156191/

Index

For the benefit of digital users, indexed terms that span two pages (e.g., 52–53) may, on occasion, appear on only one of those pages.